D0802863

Celine Dion:
Behind The Fairytale

...a Very, Very, Unauthorized Biography

by
Ian Halperin

An Original Publication of:
BOCA PUBLICATIONS GROUP, INC.
7000 West Palmetto Park Rd., suite 400
Boca Raton, FL, USA, 33433

ISBN: 0-965-95830-2

First Printing September 1997

Printed in Canada

Acknowledgements:

CONCEPT / EDITING by Esmond Choueke

JACKET DESIGN by Vadim Baboutin

LINE EDITOR Catherine Arno

PHOTOS copyright 1997 by Esmond Choueke
  / Boca Publications Group, Inc.

The author wishes to thank Burt MacFarlane for the
  use of his extensive archives and interviews.

For information, please write to:
BOCA PUBLICATIONS GROUP, INC.
7000 West Palmetto Park Rd., suite 400
Boca Raton, FL, USA, 33433

CONTENTS
(PHOTOS P.97-102)

Introduction

When I was first approached to write a book about Celine Dion almost a year ago, I had mixed feelings. As a musician and journalist in the Montreal music scene, I had crossed paths with the amazing Canadian diva several times over the years, and we had many friends in common.

I always felt somewhat uneasy with what I observed on the occasions when I was offered a glimpse inside her world. She seemed to be a wonderful person who had success thrust upon her too soon and too quickly to avoid the inevitable side effects. And, it was disconcerting to see her handlers - including her husband/manager - cynically manipulating her life and career to fit into a predetermined fairytale.

I remember meeting Celine at a Montreal press conference and telling her about a sick little girl I knew who begged me for her autograph. Without hesitation, Celine came to the edge of the stage and graciously wrote a personalized note for her. As Celine wrote, I saw in her eyes her genuine sincerity and warmth of heart.

That incident has always stayed with me, even after delving Behind The Fairytale.

Ian Halperin
September, 1997

1

Celine - Behind the Scenes at the Atlanta Olympics

It's several hours before the opening of the XXVIth Olympic Games. High above the Atlanta Olympic Stadium the flags of the 197 participating nations stirred in the humid Atlanta breeze. Dozens of technicians, promoters, security personnel, roadies and hangers-on are scrambling around the field surface during the preshow soundcheck. They're making sure there won't be any surprise glitches when the show begins with 83,000 people in the stadium and a record TV audience of 3.5 billion. Above them all, in the empty seats, Celine Dion and her husband/manager Rene Angelil are sporting sunglasses and talking to several people.

Celine, entranced and excited, notices opera star Jessye Norman warming up her voice onstage. Within hours, Celine herself - just a smalltown girl from a tiny village in Quebec, Canada - would have the honor of belting out the Olympic theme song in front of the whole world.

"Oh Rene, this is the biggest event we could ever imagine!" she says, looking as nervous as she did when she sang for the first time in public some 18 years ago. "Thanks, my darling, for getting me this show... it's a dream come true!"

Rene, joyous, and with huge beads of sweat running down his shiny forehead, kisses Celine on the cheek and says, "we did it, Cherie, we did it. Tonight every TV in the entire world will be showing you open the Olympics. Who would have ever thought that after all we've been through together that we'd be standing here tonight with a Sony recording contract and playing the biggest event in the universe!"

The road to the Olympics for Celine, however, was not strewn with roses. Her long work days and her frequent harried tours left her in a perpetual state of near exhaustion. Friends always asked her how she managed to keep at it. "Thank God I have so much energy," she'd reply. But too often now, that energy threatened to desert her. On her days off, she'd sleep eleven to fifteen hours a day. And with Rene out at business meetings to arrange future tours and appearances for hours on end, she'd be endlessly lonely and dissatisfied, stuck in a hotel room or in their Florida mansion. When he'd come home late at night Celine or Rene - or both of them - would be too tired and beat to make love or even to be good companions.

Their marriage had become a roller-coaster ride with the deepest lows and very short highs. And, as the master of her career, Rene controlled Celine's personal and professional life like a puppet master.

"I was shocked that Rene didn't give her more time off before the Olympics," says a close friend of Dion's. "Rene was working her to the bone and every time she complained of fatigue he'd make her feel guilty and say that he was working twice as hard as her arranging gigs and getting her favorable press.

"The Olympics was obviously the biggest event of Celine's career, but when I saw her the week before she left for Atlanta, she looked like she was almost near death. I had never seen her that pale before. She looked as though she had aged almost 25 years."

What even Celine did not know during the months preceding the Olympics was that Rene kept her in perpetual motion in part to avoid facing the fact that their marriage was crumbling. It wasn't because Rene was so busy and Celine was so often tired. Rene had come to resent rather than enjoy Celine's frequent attempts at domesticity, and he took to goading his wife to "act like more of a celebrity." Rene's reactions ranged from secret drinking, gambling binges, late nights out with his pals, sexual withdrawal, and throwing things around their home, according to a friend.

"Rene gets violent at times to take out his frustrations," says Dion's close friend. "Celine wanted to be a simple housewife and have kids. Rene obviously had other plans. And because their relationship was not that rosy at this time, Rene decided to increase Celine's workload twofold so she would not have any time to think about how bad the situation had actually become."

Rene and Celine's sex life often dropped to nil, and Celine worried that Rene was becoming impotent. It was only a year earlier that rumors surfaced about Rene going to a Los Angeles fertility clinic in order to try to fulfil Celine's dream of having kids. Talk of divorce was ripe around the Quebec media and paparazzi scene, but Celine and Rene were always able to band together and put on a unified front before the media.

"Rene and I have never been happier," she said. "We're just working very hard this year and after the Olympics we'll continue to tour, and soon after we'll start planning our family - right after Christmas, early in the new year."

It was a refrain that Celine would repeat often, even as

the months and years went by with her pregnancy dreams unfulfilled.

As the rehearsal for the sophisticated fireworks display continued in the Olympic Stadium, it was Celine's turn to do a sound check. Gladys Knight had just finished rehearsing *Georgia on My Mind* and she briefly talked to Celine before Celine took the microphone. Celine became more nervous. Her left hand was shaking like a leaf. She knew that this evening's performance was crucial. When one of the stage crew told her that President Clinton would speak before her performance she looked as if she was going to pass out. Reality set in. All the pre-Olympic talk, excitement and optimism meant nothing now. It was time for Celine to come up with a brilliant performance.

The Estefan Fiasco

Onstage, Celine greeted the 100-person choir. She told one member that she still could not believe that the Olympic organizers chose her over every other major recording artist for the theme song - especially the American singers. It was no wonder that Celine still couldn't believe she was the chosen one. It was only a couple of months earlier that she became enmeshed in a cauldron of anger and jealousy with fellow Sony recording artist Gloria Estefan. Estefan was so sure that she would sing at the opening ceremonies that her management booked the start of a worldwide tour the night before the July 19 ceremonies. A spokeswoman for Estefan's management company said that Estefan wanted to use the night before the opening ceremonies as a dress rehearsal.

Estefan, famous for her Latin-inspired music with The

Miami Sound Machine, was furious when she eventually found out that Olympic officials didn't choose her to sing the opening song. And, she was especially miffed because she had actually written and recorded a song about the Games that was already getting heavy airplay in the US. Like Celine, Estefan is managed by her own husband, Emilio. He threatened Sony Music that they'd pull out of their recording contract if Sony didn't force the Olympic organizers to reverse their decision. Estefan was embarrassed and angered by the snub. The fact that her main rival Dion was not even from the U.S. added insult to injury. But the protests of Estefan and her husband fell on deaf ears. Celine, the world's biggest-selling recording star, was firmly in place.

To this very day, the fur continues to fly as Estefan maintains her grudge against Celine herself for not volunteering to give her senior a chance to open the Games in front of her compatriots.

"If the Games were in Canada I would have stepped aside and given Celine the chance," Estefan said. "Celine knew how much it meant to me to open the Games in front of my fellow Americans. She also knew about all the personal turmoil that I had gone through in the last couple of years. It would have been a very classy thing for her to do.

"Instead, when I complained about being snubbed, Celine's people tried to typecast me as a troublemaker. And Sony had to take her side because she was their top-selling artist at the time. But Celine should have realized that if not for women like me who struggled for so many years to open more opportunities for female singers, she would have no career today," Estefan said.

After Estefan's team tried to get the decision reversed,

a power-struggle broke out in the Sony offices between both camps. Estefan, who records on Sony's Epic label, told people that Celine's management was typecasting Celine as the sweet, innocent character who could not refuse the offer to open the Games, but it was all baloney. She also said that she was pissed off because several of Celine's people were complaining that she (Estefan) was a bitch.

Don Mischer, executive producer of the opening and closing ceremonies in Atlanta quickly stepped in and tried to resolve the situation by offering Estefan the stage at the closing ceremonies. At first Estefan refused and threatened to have nothing at all to do with the Games. She later changed her mind when Mischer called her personally and pleaded with her to change her mind "so we can all be happy and get a piece of the action."

Mischer said he liked Estefan's song but was more blown away by Dion's version of *The Power of the Dream*, written for the event by David Foster and Linda Thompson.

"Dion's extraordinary voice and the combined talents of everyone involved in the song will make this piece a memorable part of the ceremony," Mischer said upon making his final decision. "The song is a gripping, emotional ballad that will help create the sense of drama we need to grab the world's attention."

Shortly after the committee's final announcement, a nervous Celine said "I'll make sure I have people surrounding me, supporting me, and making sure I'm not forgetting my words."

Atlanta welcomed the world and officially opened the Olympic Games with tremendous pomp and ceremony. Gladys Knight emerged out of a trapdoor in the stadium floor to sing *Georgia on My Mind*, and legendary boxer

Muhammad Ali climbed up to light the Olympic torch to officially open the Games. Celine, in such noble company, felt stomach pains and cramps before her performance. She drank a few bottles of mineral water in the hours before going onstage. Rene held her hand, telling her non-stop that nothing could go wrong and that this show would be worth millions of dollars to her career.

Finally, Celine, dressed magnificently in white, got up on stage and belted out *The Power of the Dream* with 100 musicians and 300 backup singers. "Feel the flame forever burn / Teaching lessons we must learn," she sang. "To bring us closer to the power of the dream / The world unites in hope and peace / Pray that it always will be / it is the power of the dream that brings us here."

Just minutes before she appeared onstage, there was still a lot of talk behind her back. NBC-TV said, "Celine is making all Canadians proud tonight, but we're still surprised that she was chosen over all the American singers."

Celine's performance got mixed reviews. Most called it satisfactory, but her press was awful. "Still in the throes of a bad-hair year," Jack Todd of The Montreal Gazette wrote the next day, "Celine Dion sang a David Foster tune with Linda Thompson lyrics so corny they would embarrass the clog dancers at a pick-up picnic."

But the triumph was evident: she was the chosen one over all the other divas in the world.

The next day Celine received congratulatory telegrams from hordes of friends and associates. But she felt exhausted and was not looking forward to the next few months of touring. She realized that her relentless drive to the top was exacting a heavy price on her health and personal life.

2

The Child Star Who Never Had a Childhood

Therese Dion was rushed to the hospital on a freezing cold Saturday night to have her fourteenth child. When she gave birth, she named her daughter after a Hughes Auffray song which she loved that had played frequently during her pregnancy, *Celine*. Celine Dion was born at 12:30 AM on March 30, 1968.

Celine was one of Therese's largest baby girls, weighing eight pounds, eight ounces at birth. Therese never could have imagined that her baby daughter, who was so happy and healthy, would develop a severe eating disorder and look like skin and bones before she reached 16.

As Therese and Adhemar Dion saw Celine's features develop, they realized that the baby of their family would, inevitably, be beautiful. As their newest and last baby, they always kept Celine within arm's reach, keeping her to themselves as much as possible. They'd encourage her 13 brothers and sisters to play with her and take care of her, almost to the total exclusion of the companionship of other children her own age. To keep Celine's mind occupied when they were alone, Therese would read French fairytales out loud to her, nourishing a fantasy life within her, according to one of her early school teachers.

"Perhaps it would have been healthier and more normal for Celine to play in the sandbox with other boys and girls and their toys rather than hearing fairytales for hundreds of hours - but that was how the Dions wanted it," her teacher said. "She was rarely allowed to mix with children her age."

Celine's Family Tree

Celine's musical roots stretch at least 300 years back to the time when her ancestors sailed to America from France and settled in Quebec. On both sides of her family, Celine's heritage courses back through the centuries to these early pioneers. Two of the earliest were Jean Guyon and his wife Mathurine Robin, who sailed from Mortagne in the Province of Perche in the mid 1600s to explore the riches of the new world. This marriage produced ten children.

One descendant, Jean Guyon-DuBuisson, married in November of 1645, and this marriage produced a son named Pierre Guyon, who became the first person in the large family to take on a new spelling of their name - Dion.

Celine's ancestors in the 1600s sang and were very interested in music, mainly because it was a way to relieve the hardship and squalor of their early years in America. Their music expressed their sentiments about having left their mother country and eking out a living in France's new land, Quebec.

Celine's own grandparents and parents struggled as farmers in Quebec's scenic Gaspe region. Celine's father, Adhemar Dion, was born March 2, 1923 into a family of five boys and two girls. Her mom, Therese Tanguay, was born four years later on March 20,1927, the sixth of nine children.

Therese and Adhemar were from very similar backgrounds, part of the dirt poor working class trying to gain economic and social stability. Even though they grew up beside each other in the same village of Sainte Anne-des-Monts, Therese and Adhemar barely knew each other.

Tough economic times forced both their families to abandon their farms and move to a bigger city to look for work. Adhemar's family had been on the brink of starvation before they finally decided to sell their farm and move. Coincidentally, both Adhemar and Therese's family wound up in La Tuque, and the two ended up meeting one night because they jammed together at an improvised music session!

Therese, who grew up constantly singing and tinkering with various instruments around the house, was playing a popular Quebec folk song *Le Reel de Sainte Anne* on the violin. Adhemar, who also grew up wanting to be a musician, got up and accompanied her on the accordion. When their eyes met for the first time, it was love at first sight.

Ten months later, on June 20, 1945, Therese and Adhemar exchanged marriage vows at the St. Zephirin church, and a year later, on August 15, Therese gave birth to their first child, Denise.

Historically, Catholic families in Quebec produced many offspring, and so did the marriage of Celine's parents, who were both staunch believers. In fact, Adhemar was not crazy about the idea of having so many children. "As long as we can have two or three healthy children, I'd be more than happy," he often told Therese.

By the mid 1950's, Therese had given birth to four children and was pregnant with a fifth. Once gain, severe financial problems placed the couple in a really bad situation. Adhemar was struggling to put enough food on the table to feed the hungry little mouths under his roof. When Therese got pregnant for the fifth time, Adhemar desperately began searching for work in other towns. The family wound up moving to a small town just outside Quebec City called Charlemagne where Celine was eventually born. Adhemar had found a job working in a factory, where he'd often put in 16-18 hours a day to make ends meet. When he got home late at night, he'd often be too tired to even eat and would crash almost instantly in the tiny apartment the Dions rented.

Even though things were better financially in Charlemagne, Therese missed living on the farm. She also didn't want her children to grow up in utter squalor, so she decided to save every penny she had for the next few years to buy another farm.

Adhemar saved 40 cents every day by walking several miles to work instead of paying the 20-cent bus fare each way. Even when he had the flu or felt very tired, he would never give in to the temptation to take the bus and would hand over the 40 cents to Therese at the end of each day. Therese saved the money in a big cookie jar.

To the amazement of their friends and neighbors, most of whom were also struggling, the Dions eventually put down $400 to buy a small piece of land in Charlemagne. The only problem was that they didn't have any extra money to buy a house. Therese and Adhemar soon decided to build a house with their own hands.

Pregnant with her seventh child in 1954, Therese astonished her neighbors by climbing daily up the ladder with a hammer to help build her family home. Adhemar would sleep sometimes not more than two hours a night as he combined his job with building a home. Sometimes he would still be hammering at 4 AM, only two hours before he had to leave for work.

"We built the house all by ourselves," recalled Therese. "Our family was growing fast and we wanted to give our children the chance to live in a comfortable home and not wind up sleeping on top of one another. We even installed the heating system. We were so broke in those days because times were tough and we had a lot of little mouths to feed. The neighbors were shocked when they regularly saw me and my husband climbing up ladders and hammering away."

When their house was finished, the Dions managed to rise above the squalor which plagued so many families in Charlemagne. The moderate home dazzled with Therese's homey decor. Whoever visited the Dions would immediately feel right at home. The aroma of Therese's cooking permeated the household and happy little children were everywhere. Adhemar started making more money and the Dion household filled with a fairytale-like atmosphere.

Therese and Adhemar decided to use their musical talents to earn extra income. They formed a group and played at various parties and weddings. Meanwhile, Celine, who was several years younger than her closest sibling, became the darling of her older brother and sisters. They would play with her endlessly, take her on walks, and buy her special gifts.

"Celine loved performing for us. I remember one time when she was only four years old and she got up on our table and started to imitate a singer and dancer. She was so cute - but also very accurate. She'd move her tiny little arms around just like she was really on a stage. And, she insisted on picking up a fork or spoon to use as a microphone!" says Claudette, who also is Celine's godmother.

On another occasion, one of her sisters put sunglasses on her and took her to a 30-cent photo machine for a treat to get a few small pictures taken with her. Celine was definitely the darling of the family.

Claudette adds that, "all of Celine's clothes were hand-me-downs from all the other sisters which our mother would fix up for her. Therese would spend hours altering the dresses the older daughters wore to make them really pretty for Celine. I still remember the beautiful pink dress mom sewed from scratch for Celine's first TV appearance when she was 12 years old. She looked gorgeous! Mom was always Celine's biggest booster."

Claudette also revealed that, "Celine always said her dream and goal was to become a star - and that she actually believes it's a destiny that God wants for her..."

Celine uttered her first word when she was only nine months old. "Dan" she said, referring to her older brother Daniel, who she used to play with regularly. Her first sentence was "Mama, je t'aime"... (" Mom, I love you.")

Celine was her mother's pride and joy. Therese would spend hours on end teaching Celine to speak and to sing by age three. Celine's efforts to win Adhemar's attention were not as successful. He was preoccupied in spending time with his sons, teaching them to play ice hockey and baseball, and how to swim. He only spent time with his daughters at family sing-alongs or when one of them needed a scolding for doing poorly in school or for staying out too late at night.

Celine's Career Begins

When she reached the age of three, Celine started to emulate the rest of her family and sang traditional folk songs. Celine's brothers and sisters would teach her the words to several well-known songs and Celine would try to sing along. Despite not being able to pronounce most of the lyrics properly, Celine's family was convinced that their youngest member had music in her blood.

"She could hold a tune ever since she started talking," her mother bragged. "And she had good pitch. She always sang in the right key. I knew that my daughter might become a musician right away because she always smiled when she sang. And when she sang, anybody who heard her fell in love with her instantly. She had a way to make people smile and forget their problems."

Therese and Adhemar decided to open a family restaurant and piano bar, Le Vieux Baril, a business that would enable them to incorporate music into their daily routine. Some of Celine's fondest early memories occurred in Le Vieux Baril, which flourished for years under the Dions.

"Our clientele was mainly regular people," says Therese. "I worked the restaurant preparing meals and my husband worked serving alcohol to the customers. It was an intimate bar and we avoided having undesirable people. We never got into trouble because of drunk people or drugs."

Therese says the nicest gift she ever received was a violin her father bought her at Eaton's department store when she was a kid. So, when Celine was born, Adhemar rushed out to buy his wife a new violin because he thought that at age 40, Therese was still young enough to continue her music career - and she played it often at Le Vieux Baril.

By the time she was only five, Celine began performing there regularly. Customers got a kick at how Celine dressed up like singers that she had seen perform on television. The young girl would imitate her favorite singers and the audience would react with laughter and huge applause. They sometimes threw $10 bills at her feet to show their appreciation - a huge amount of money at the time.

Claudette said that Celine's first public performance was at their brother Michel's wedding. Michel, who now works for Celine full-time arranging her concert tours, was a singer himself for over 20 years under his stage name Michel St. Clair.

"Celine captured everybody's heart at Michel's wedding by singing so beautifully. We were in awe about how amazing she was. It was at that point that we all knew she could become a famous singer," Claudette added.

Celine performed three songs at the wedding, including Roger Whittaker's famous *Mammy Blue*.

In fact, all of Celine's 13 brothers and sisters dabbled in music for brief periods. They played guitar, drums, bass and sang.

"Our family would sing together all the time while my father played accordion," recalls Celine's sister Claudette. "Even though we weren't rich, we were still happy because we expressed our feelings with music. When the children in our family started to cry or if someone was depressed, my father would take out his accordion and the whole family would be happy again."

Life around the Dion family's new home was almost idyllic. Little Celine was free to roam with her older brothers and sisters because there wasn't too much traffic on their quiet street. Celine loved growing up around lots of greenery and she would often ask her mother for breadcrumbs to feed the birds.

But Celine's childhood was marred by an accident that came close to killing her when she was five - and which would leave emotional scars for her whole life. When she was playing in front of her parents' house on Notre-Dame Street, she noticed a baby carriage across the street. Celine, who loved playing with little babies, began crossing the street despite being warned repeatedly by her parents to "never cross the street alone".

The mother of the baby across the street began yelling at Celine not to cross - and Celine stopped still, standing frozen in the middle of the street wondering what to do. She then headed back towards her house. That was when a big truck backed out of the supermarket across the street from Celine's home and slammed into her. Celine did a back flip in the air and landed right on her head.

Her brother Michel heard the commotion and ran into the middle of the street to get his younger sister who was lying there unconscious. He rushed Celine to the hospital where she lay motionless in the intensive care unit for more than two days. It took months for Celine to fully recuperate from her severely fractured skull. Doctors warned the Dion family that they were not sure whether Celine would ever fully recuperate from the blow.

"It was the most devastating time in our lives," Claudette told a reporter. "Our beloved sister lay in the hospital and there was nothing any of us could do. We all prayed for her and just hoped that she would pull through."

"I'll never forget her accident," added her father Adhemar. "Usually, during the day, my wife and my children never let Celine out of their sight. This was the only time she was out alone because something was going on in our house. I almost had a heart attack when I was told what happened. Luckily Celine pulled through - we would never have forgiven themselves if something happened to her."

Even as an adult approaching 30, Celine still seems to retain a fearful memory of that accident, as she rarely ventures out on the street without her husband or a companion beside her. She also complains of frequent migraine headaches and nausea, which may stem from be the aftereffects of this horrifying accident.

The young Céline refused to cross the street without the aid of an adult for several years after her accident. Even today, when Celine is on the busy streets of Manhattan, Paris or Montreal, she looks both ways several times before crossing.

"One time when we were in London, Celine didn't realize that the cars went the other way," recalls one of her back-up musicians. "She started crossing the street and almost got hit by a taxi. You should have seen the poor girl's face. She froze and seemed to be having a panic attack. Then she told us about her accident as a child. It must have had quite an effect on her because she is always looking over her shoulder wherever she goes."

Obviously, the trauma of the accident has remained with her to the present day. She expresses her paranoid fears of her own possible death, and always needs to have someone like her husband or bodyguard by her side to protect her, a band member says.

When Celine finally recuperated, her brothers and sisters didn't let her out of their sight for months. They would even take turns driving her to school and picking her up every day.

Although Celine was a little angel then, her brothers and sisters were already engaging in mischief. When she was seven years old, she scolded her older brother Jacques for buying a pack of cigarets, according to one of her brothers.

"It's no good for you," she told him when she caught him smoking in the back of their house. "Don't do that because our mom will get mad!"

Therese remembers that she always thought Celine's singing was just a phase. "She was so young and she would always want to sing," Therese said.

"But I never thought it would turn into something serious because I saw all of my other children grow up with music and then go into other things. When she was only six years old, I surprised her by writing a love song and we sang it together all the time. I really enjoyed teaching Celine music."

The new Dion restaurant / piano-bar became instantly popular in Charlemagne. People would dine, drink and then join a sing-a-long until the early hours of the morning. Celine was a huge attraction in the bar and men used to show their appreciation by throwing money at her feet while she sang. But some patrons of the bar were shocked and outraged to see the underage Celine become a regular fixture there.

"The Dions were a very nice Quebecois family," recalls Pierre Tremblay, a Charlemagne resident who used to drink regularly at Le Vieux Baril.

"Even though little Celine stole the show whenever she got up to sing, I couldn't believe that her family would let her be in a room surrounded by smoke and alcohol. Instead of being at home studying or being in bed by 9 PM, Celine would be helping out her family in the bar and would get up and sing. If something like that happened today, the family would have child welfare groups on their backs immediately."

By the time Celine was nine years old, her parents were convinced that Celine was destined for the stage. So they encouraged her to hang out in their bar.

"I had to let her in the bar to sing or else she would cry," said her mother. "When I saw her around the house, she was often unhappy because she wanted to come to our bar and sing for the crowd. From the first time she got up to sing in front of people at age five, I realized that Celine needed to touch people with her voice.

"That first time she received a huge ovation I realized that Celine had the heart and soul of a true artist."

The festive atmosphere of Le Vieux Baril encouraged Celine to go home and practice singing in front of the mirror so that she would improve her performance each time she got up to sing in the bar. While her friends played with Barbie dolls or hung out at the local candy store, Celine practiced in front of the mirror sometimes up to eight hours a day. She would practice singing and dancing to some of her favorite tunes of Quebec star Ginette Reno.

From her earliest memories, the little girl Celine always felt compelled to entertain people.

"I knew from when I was a tiny skinny girl that singing was for me," Celine recalls. "I loved bringing out emotions in people with my voice. To this day, the biggest thrill in life for me is to move people with my voice."

By the age of ten, Celine had become a true local celebrity. People flocked to her parents' bar to hear her sing. And when she was not there, the locals would constantly request to Therese and Adhemar that they call Celine at home and ask her to rush to the bar to entertain the crowd.

"It was difficult because everybody wanted to hear Celine sing and often she was already in bed sleeping," Therese said. "A lot of people might think that we shouldn't have let our daughter sing in a bar at that age but we had no choice. Celine was a hit and you have to give customers what they request."

Because of this singing, Celine's grades suffered. Although she passed most of her classes, she never lived up to the potential that most of her teachers thought she possessed. At best she was an average student. A couple of her teachers complained to her parents that she was growing up around bad influences.

One of Celine's former teachers at L'Ecole St. Jude recalled, "a lot of times Celine showed up at school looking like she hadn't slept the night before.

"She was a quiet girl who didn't get into much trouble but she had the potential to be a scholar if her parents encouraged her more. Even though she had musical talent, it didn't mean that she should be out in bars late at night entertaining people at least three times her age," her teacher said.

"Because she had so many older brothers and sisters, Celine felt that she always had to hang around older people. She had a few friends in the class but she was a bit withdrawn."

Sometimes Celine fell so far behind in school that her brothers and sisters did her homework for her.

"We helped her with her studies because she was a busy girl combining music and school," said Celine's sister Manon. "Celine was a quiet kid and always polite. But she never got to be more than an average student because she was always dreaming about becoming a singing star."

At ten, Celine started to draw the attention of several people in the music business. She covered many songs including several by her idol Ginette Reno. Word spread to Montreal that there was a little gem moving people with her voice at Le Vieux Baril. By now Celine's parents realized that their youngest child was destined to have a career on stage, but they were nervous about the music business.

"When she started to become popular in Charlemagne, I felt like I always had to protect her," said her mother. "We didn't think she was ready for anything more than singing in our club because she was so young. And she only sang cover tunes and most agents want to hear original songs. So we decided that if the right offer came along, we would consider it. Until then we wanted Celine to be patient and to just continue getting better."

But too many people kept telling Therese that Celine was a child prodigy and that she could be the biggest thing to ever come out of Quebec. Even in the supermarket, everybody would ask Therese how her talented young daughter was doing. Celine's siblings encouraged her parents to speed up their sister's young career.

"Mama, we must do something now because she is so good," said her brother Jacques. "Maybe we should put together some original music for Celine and send it off to the right people. We could make a fortune."

Jacques' words of wisdom would affect the Dions' lives forever. Therese spoke at length with Adhemar and decided to seek out an agent to handle Celine's career. That was the turning point in Celine's life. She would soon become familiar to thousands of Quebecers and be the next child singing sensation in "La Belle Province". But Celine's road to fame would not be without many obstacles that would make her almost want to quit the music business, no matter how much she loved music itself.

3

The Agent Who Discovered Celine
(No, It Wasn't Rene!)

A novelist would be hard pressed to invent a career start more implausible than that of Celine Dion. It is a story of public acclaim and private tragedy, of traumatic injury and obstinate recovery. In addition to music, the story embraces political intrigue and financial scandal and often seems to be a panorama too vast to be encompassed within anybody's lifetime.

The launching of Celine's career was not easy. That is clear from the most casual perusal of her past. From age ten, Dion's life has been an improbable spree of accomplishment and chaos, progress and inconsistency, mastery and drift. But the way she got her start sounds clear and simple if you believe the fable that she and her spin doctors continually feed the press - they always say that Rene discovered her and became her agent when she was 12.

"The way they tell the fairytale story about how she was discovered is just something they use to make people love her," says an insider. "But it's obviously not true."

In fact, nobody talks about the man who really did discover Celine because no outsider even knows his name anymore. The name which has been lost to rock history is Paul Levesque, Celine's first agent and discoverer, who was paid off by Rene to sail silently into the sunset in the early 1980s.

The official story, as related by Celine, Rene, and everyone else in their family and entourage, including her publicist, hairdresser, dressmaker, throat doctor, and so on, sounds like this:

"When I was 12, my mother and I sought out Rene to be my agent, because he was the best there was in Quebec. We knew I couldn't get any farther in my career without a good agent. To make sure he'd notice me, my mom and I made a demo tape and she helped me wrap it up with a big red ribbon... ," Celine will say.

"I was so nervous when he finally called to make an appointment, and I walked into his office... I began singing into a pen, pretending it was a microphone, to show him how I sing. Rene actually cried from his emotions, and he quickly told us that one day I'd be singing for the whole world. Of course, we didn't believe it, but he did agree to represent me," Celine continues.

"I always thought I was meant to be a singer... but I had no idea how far I'd be able to go... all my success now is due to him, and the fact that he discovered me and led my career..." Celine will say.

* * * * *

If you were cruising along the outskirts of Laval in the late 1970s and saw what appeared to be a sports car dealership, chances were good that you stumbled upon the parking lot of the home of Quebec rock manager Paul Levesque. Levesque is a name that can forever conjure up the worst excesses in Quebec rock'n roll history for those who knew him 'way back when. He was known for throwing expensive wild parties while on the road with his clients, buying his artists fancy sports cars, and for spending huge amounts on clothes. Legend has it that he once spent over $20,000 on a fur coat and which he still has never tried on!

Like many self-employed entrepreneurs, Levesque was obsessed. He worked virtually all the time, mostly in his office which he now operates out of his eclectically decorated home in Rosemere, a suburb about 40 miles north of Montreal. Levesque says he still manages to party but the long intensive hours involved in trying to promote his current stars often makes it difficult these days. And, the successes now seem far behind...

Some of the artists in Levesque's stable over the years included heavy rock giants Mahogany Rush, top 40 songstress Luba, and Quebec franco-rocker Bruno Pelletier. All are now forgotten. But the one artist whom he talks most animatedly about and the one whom he still kicks himself in the head for losing is Quebec's Queen - Celine.

"I guess I let her get away..." he says disparagingly.

Levesque is compact and spare with his emotions, except when it comes to Celine. He contradicts all reports from Celine's camp about how she was really discovered - and he temper rises whenever he discusses Rene.

"I'm the one who discovered Celine and first signed her - and all those other reports about Rene discovering her are false," stresses Levesque.

"I signed her when she was only 11, and it was me who introduced her to Rene a year later!"

Levesque recalls the day in the late 1970s when a carpenter who was working on his new house urged him to go scout "a skinny girl with crooked teeth who could sing up a storm." Levesque was initially very sceptical, thinking that it would be ridiculous to try to market an 11-year-old waiflike adult contemporary singer in a market dominated by French-speaking veterans Marjo and Ginette Reno. One night, however, Celine was singing in a local piano bar and Levesque decided to go. He says that he got slightly intoxicated on the way to Celine's gig but "sobered up quickly" the minute he heard her sing her first note.

"I got goosebumps all over me," recalls Levesque. "And that's the way I decide whether or not to sign an artist. My measuring stick is that if an artist gives me goosebumps, I pursue them."

That night, Levesque went over to Celine's parents in the audience and immediately made them a contract offer. By the end of the evening, the smooth-talking manager and the Dion family reached a verbal agreement for him to control Celine's career.

"Whenever I read about Rene discovering Celine I think to myself what a bunch of bull it is", says Levesque. "It was even me who sent Celine's demo tape to Rene - and if not for me she wouldn't have had a career. And I guess no marriage either."

Levesque was fascinated by the exuberance and drive of Celine. He worked her to the bone in their first year together, sometimes doing shopping mall appearances in the day, radio appearances in the afternoon and performing in clubs at night. But he was unsuccessful in his persistent attempts to land her a recording contract.

"I knocked on every door out there," he remembers. "But nobody wanted to take a chance on her. The Quebec market has always been a tight clique and it's tough to break in new artists. And because Celine was only 11 that made it more difficult."

Though Levesque barely knew Rene before sending him Celine's demo tape, the two men began to grow close immediately. After hearing the demo, Rene called Levesque right away and asked him to set up a meeting. He told Levesque that he had the connections to make Celine a mega star in Quebec, and the two of them should join forces. Levesque, who was flirting with bankruptcy by then, jumped at Rene's offer. He immediately phoned Celine's mom and told her that he had finally generated interest in young Celine. He noodled over the possibility of accompanying Celine to Rene's office but thought it would be less formal if Celine went with her mom, and set up the meeting.

"That's one of the important things that all the Dions seem to have conveniently forgotten when they tell their tale about their package with the red ribbon on it," Levesque says.

The relationship between the Dions and Levesque up till this time had started to become complicated. Celine's parents were becoming concerned that the too-smooth manager was incapable of handling a child star. Many times Levesque was intoxicated or stoned around Celine, a habit that was of great concern to the entire family.

"Paul went through his bout of drug and alcohol problems around the time he managed Celine," recalls a Montreal record producer. "I knew that his relationship with Celine would be shortlived. He didn't have any idea what to do with Celine's talent."

The most controversial part of Levesque, however, was his propensity to promise the world to Celine, most of which he would never fulfil. "He had the kid believing she was the next best thing since sliced bread," recalls the musician. "Celine obviously did not know Paul well. Anybody who has ever worked for him knows that he's 99.9% cheap talk."

Untll Levesque managed to get Rene to take notice of young Celine, he was debating what to do with his child prodigy. Celine remained an asset in many ways, even though she was not getting the same attention as other Quebec stars. She was overwhelmingly popular among rural Quebecers. Her gigs in smalltown locations such as Laval, Victoriaville and Chicoutimi won raves. Bit by bit Celine moved up the Quebec pop music ladder. But Levesque could not manage to get a record label to take notice. After a series of confessed errors of judgement in dealing with Celine's career, Levesque new it was time to do something.

"With a child star you have to move fast or they start to become adults in the eyes of the public," says Levesque. "When Rene expressed interest in Celine I had to make a deal. He had contacts in television and lots of contacts with record labels. If I would not have got Rene involved we still might be looking to this day at how to get Celine a contract."

As legend has it, Rene became infatuated with Celine at first glance. Even during their first meeting with Celine's mother present, Rene stared continuously into young Celine's eyes. This made Celine uncomfortable. The little girl couldn't return Rene's stare. She turned her head continuously at her mother and pretended not to notice Rene's continuous gazing. Celine's mother struck up a conversation with Rene about Quebec singer Ginette Reno, who at the time was Rene's big client. Rene told Therese about how Ginette played clubs and concert halls for years without a recording contract. He promised that would not be the case with Celine and that he'd "make Celine a star within five years." Celine and her mother laughed when they heard Rene say this.

"All that I want is for Celine to be happy and have the chance to make a bit of money," Therese said. "If you think you can help us, we'd be glad to work with you."

Rene was fascinated by the fact that Levesque had been unable to do much with such a talent. An enmity was born between the two men when Levesque found out that Rene was badmouthing him behind his back to Celine's family. Privately, Rene told his wife Anne that Levesque was "a jerk" and that , "I'll soon get this idiot out of the way to take full control of what Paul Levesque almost ruined."

Rene and Levesque worked out an agreement to have Rene manage and promote Celine's career. Rene also signed Celine to his independent label TBS Records. Levesque, however, still kept a marketing and promotional role in Celine's career. But tempers got quickly out of hand in the first year of their business relations. The hard feelings intensified when Rene began to suspect that Levesque was allowing himself to be unduly influenced by the pattern of other Quebec artists. He found no logical pattern to the songs that Levesque chose for Celine to work the hardest. After only a few months, Rene would not even let Celine go anywhere near Levesque. He instructed the Dion family not to return any of Levesque's phone calls. But Rene forgot to take into account the capriciousness of Paul Levesque.

Levesque was stung by Rene's criticism and began badmouthing him to the press. "I introduced him to her and now that he sees the talent I was talking about, he wants her all to himself," he once told a French radio interviewer. "We differ in the whole outlook of things. If I would have known how this man would let his ego take over, I would never have sent him the demo tape of Celine. I feel that he's trying to manipulate Celine in order to rip me off."

Levesque's growing rift with Rene was not his only problem. Several of his other artists, including rock band Mahogany Rush, were becoming increasingly discontented with his work. Levesque was starting to find it hard to calm his recalcitrant group of artists. He also harbored an inferiority complex about being number two to Rene. So when Rene approached him in 1980 about being bought out of Dion's career, he quickly accepted. It was a decision he would greatly regret.

"If I would have known then how far Celine could go, I would have never sold out for the price I did (less than $50,000)," Levesque says. "Let's face it, not one artist I've ever touched can slightly compare to the success Celine has enjoyed.

"I knew Rene was capable of helping her career but I never thought that he would make her this big. Let's face it - Rene was a big fish in a small pond at the time and with no experience in the world scheme of things in music. But later on when he got the company Sony behind the project everything changed. If I would have known that Sony would get involved, it would have taken a lot more money to buy me out because I'm the guy who discovered Celine. I was also the first person in the world to take a chance on her. Oh well, that's the music business - win some lose some."

* * * * *

Perhaps the last word in this saga should go to Celine's sister, Claudette, who recounts one of the most touching aspects of the fable - and the detail that is true, according to all accounts: their mother, Therese, actually wrote the words to the song that was presented on a cheap demo tape for Rene.

"Both Celine and our mom realized that they'd have to sing an original song to really impress such an important agent - and we certainly didn't have the money to pay a songwriter," Claudette said.

"So mom told Celine, 'I'll write you a new song!'"

"With the same determination mom used to sew Celine's dresses, she sat down with brother Jacques while he strummed a tune on the guitar, and she wrote a beautiful song for Celine, *It Was Only a dream.*

"Celine and our brother Jacques worked out a tune on the guitar, and he hummed it for mom as she toiled away with a pencil and paper, forcing herself to come up with a rhyme to fit the tune," Claudette says.

"As mom wrote more lines, Celine would sing them, and then mom would change and add words until she was satisfied... it was very moving and very inspirational," Claudette says.

"The first verse sounding like this: I found myself wandering / through an enchanted garden / a harp and violin were playing / and the angels in heaven were smiling at me / Even the winds sang of summer.

"And, the chorus went like this: It was only a dream, only a dream / but so beautiful that it must have been real / like the dawn of a new day / It was only a dream, a smile on my lips / a smile which I saved at the end of my dream."

Claudette says that their mom got hold of "a dinky $25 cassette recorder" and recorded the song in their kitchen.

"They turned on the tape recorder, and Celine sang the

words mom wrote for *It Was Only a Dream* as brother Jacques strummed the guitar," she says.

"Then, mom helped Celine find a big red ribbon to tie up the cassette before mailing it to the agent named Rene Angelil - to make sure the package would be noticed within his mail..." Claudette says.

"As always, ever since Celine began singing at church and at local get-togethers, mom and Celine discussed every possible angle about this decision - and they've continued doing that even to this day..."

Upon completion, the Dions named the song *It Was Only a Dream*. Anybody who suspects that young Celine sang without emotion at age 12 is in for a shock. In fact, her sister says it was clear in this first effort that Celine was destined to become a singer who would make the world take notice. When the whole Dion family heard the final product, Claudette says that some of them wept from early on in the first verse.

Although Claudette totally skips the part Levesque played, she continues the tale...

"Rene liked the song so much that he invited Celine down for a meeting.

"Mom - who was sewing all Celine's clothes at the time, made sure she looked really pretty in another new dress as they made the nerve-wracking trip to Angelil's office.

"Mom held Celine's hand in the car saying, 'don't be nervous Celine, and if he asks you to sing, just sing the way you always do, and he will love it...just be yourself, the way you always are...'" Claudette said.

As for Rene, he later told his associate, "I didn't know what to make of this quiet, shy kid. Her voice was the most beautiful thing I had ever heard.

"Tears actually filled my eyes at the sound of her singing. I was determined to represent her, starting immediately: I told Celine and her mother, 'trust in me, and I'll make her a giant star within five years.'

"They both believed me, and I believed it too."

* * * * *

P.S. On September 10, 1997, Forbes magazine announces that Celine is the world's most popular solo singer, having earned $ 65 million in the 1996-97 season, and ranking 15th among the world's highest-paid entertainers. The only musical groups to have earned more that season are The Rolling Stones, at $ 68 million, and The Beatles, at $ 8 million. As for Gloria Estefan, she came in 31st at $ 7million. Madonna, Barbra Streisand, and Mariah Carey don't even make it onto this Top-40 list.

4

Celine's Diabolical Svengali

Except for her parents, Rene would be the strongest influence on Celine's life and career, first as a manager and soon as a lover. He introduced Celine to everybody important in the Quebec music scene, but most of all he almost adopted Celine when he persuaded her to move into his Montreal office.

When Therese told Adhemar the news he was furious at first.

"We can't let our baby move in with a man so old," he told Therese. "Even though it might help her career she's way too young to be mingling with people in showbusiness who are so much older than her."

Therese convinced Adhemar that Rene was respectable and that he was happily married to Anne, Rene's second wife, who also helped build Celine's career in the early days. Therese assured her husband that she would accompany Celine on every road trip and would keep a very close eye on her.

"When Celine goes to Paris, Japan and across Canada I will be there with her every step of the way," Therese promised Adhemar. "I'll make sure that if her career takes off, Celine will stay the same and not get spoiled."

Another big concern was Celine's academics. Her classmates considered her charming and were very aware of her singing talent, but Celine had poor grades and fell behind quickly.

Despite the fact that Rene repeatedly promised Celine's parents that her grades wouldn't suffer, Celine dropped out of school by age 14. Many people blamed Rene for not encouraging her to stick with school at least until she graduated from high school.

"Even though Celine always wanted to be a singer I never imagined that this quiet girl would grow up to be a star," said Diane Senecal, Celine's sixth grade teacher. "I had taught some of her other brothers and sisters and I knew that the family had lots of musical talent. But I know that the music field is unstable and that education is vitally important. I didn't want her to be very disappointed if things didn't work out. It could have caused her a lot of pain."

Rene made many hefty promises to Celine and her parents when he signed on as her manager. Aside from guaranteeing Celine huge TV and print media exposure, he also promised to inject a lot of his own money to record and promote her. In fact, these promises he did eventually live up to. Rene's talk sounded awfully good to Dion family, and they agreed that she'd sign on with him But there was one big problem. Rene was broke and wasn't sure himself if he would be able to fulfil his promises.

Rene was in debt because several of his past business schemes failed miserably. And his heavy gambling drained off a lot of his funds. When Rene first approached his banker about a loan, he almost got laughed out of the building.

"Your bank account is redder than the Canadian flag," his bank manager told him.

Rene persisted and soon convinced another bank

branch to help him out. But the loan conditions were strict because Rene's bank history was erratic.

The only way the bank would loan Rene the money to finance Celine's first album would be if he mortgaged his home and got a guarantor. Rene's longtime friend Denys Bergeron who ran Trans-Canada Records, a large Quebec record distributor, agreed to endorse Rene's loan. When Rene approached his wife Anne about mortgaging their home, she was furious.

"Are you crazy?" she asked him. "We have children - and if your business scheme doesn't work, they'll wind up homeless. You haven't had much luck in business recently and now you want to blow our whole life savings on an unknown 12-year-old. I think you're losing your mind!"

Rene promised his wife that if his business plan failed he would go out and "find a regular job." Anne, who made a decent living as the star of the popular French-language TV show *Les Tannants* (*The Troublemakers*), told her husband that she would give him six months and if he was still losing money on Celine he'd have to find something else to do.

Rene finally secured the loan and got Celine into a studio to start recording. Rene decided that he would release two Celine albums simultaneously, including one Christmas album.

A dubious Anne told her husband, "Celine hasn't even sold one record and you're releasing a Christmas album for her!"

"I think that you'll be job hunting very soon, my dear."

The first thing Rene did was engage the services of legendary songwriter Eddy Marnay, who had penned songs in French for stars like Edith Piaf, Nana Mouskouri and

Michel Legrand. He also hired his longtime friend Daniel Hetu to rearrange the song written by Celine's mother *It Was Only a Dream* (*Ce N'etait Qu'un Reve*). Hetu was a well-known Quebec orchestra leader who also was the arranger for Quebec star Ginette Reno.

Rene always felt that if a singer could make an audience cry, it was a sure route to success. When he gave instructions to his new musical team, he emphasized this point. "I want you guys to write music for Celine that will bring tears to everybody's eyes. I have my whole life riding on this, so please do the best job ever. I'll take care of everybody if this gamble pays off," he said.

Meanwhile, Rene's wife, who at this point didn't have an inkling that Rene would eventually fall in love with young Celine, began teaching Celine the intricacies of performing in public and in front of TV cameras.

"Always smile and make it look simple," Anne told Celine. "Even if you don't feel well or are having a bad day you must smile because that will make your fans happy. Your smile is worth a million dollars, so use it."

Those were lessons that Celine came to remember and practice throughout her lowest periods and worst hardships - including during her up-and-down weight battles and marital wars. Always the trooper, she had an amazing inner strength which she drew on to rally herself even when she felt the worst.

On June 19, 1981, Rene decided to introduce Celine to the Quebec public. He convinced Rene-Pierre Beaudry, a researcher for Quebec's biggest TV talk show, to book his young protégé. The show's well-known host, Michel Jasmin, introduced a timid young 13-year-old Celine saying, "for the first time we would like to present to you a hot new young talent with a magnificent voice, Celine Dion."

That was the beginning of the love affair between the Celine and millions of Quebecers. Even to this day, Celine remains the most popular figure in Quebec no matter what she does. A 1997 study by a Montreal marketing firm revealed that 99.3 per cent of Quebecers could identify Ms. Dion. Another survey by Quebec's top polling firm Leger&Leger said 90 per cent of the population had only good things to say about Celine. In comparison, only 68.5 per cent had a favorable opinion of the charismatic top politician of the province, Lucien Bouchard. She began to take on an air of being local royalty.

A prominent Montreal journalist said, "it's amazing to think that somebody who's not even that intelligent and who constantly lied to the public about her private life can become such a hero. I've followed her career since the beginning and I'm still amazed at how Quebecers just swallow whatever hype they're fed from her camp."

Another well-known Montreal columnist, Nathalie Petrowski of La Presse, is also flabbergasted by Celine's continuing cherished status in her home province, and wonders what Celine has done to deserve this respect. She wrote, "all Celine and Rene know about is how to put on a show. In fact, they make a flourishing business out of it - but it's not designed to help people live better lives. The point is to maintain illusions and appearances. For years, they've lied to people about their relationship - why would they stop lying now?"

Celine's debut recording *La Voix Du Bon Dieu*, which was penned after a song Eddy Marnay wrote for her, was launched simultaneously with Celine Dion *Sings Christmas Carols* (*Chante Noel*).

Rene worked Celine hard to promote her child-star image and her debut albums. He booked her for countless TV, radio and record store appearances and even got her to do numerous shopping mall gigs. Frequently, Rene himself worked around the clock trying to promote his young artist and recoup his investment. Celine's grueling schedule had a drastic affect on her grades in school and within a year she decided to drop her studies totally. Rene didn't prevent her from dropping out, despite the fact that she hadn't even finished high school. Instead, all her energy went into becoming a star.

"Rene had a young artist who would be more than willing to get up at 7 AM and start smiling and singing for hundreds of people in shopping malls," said Montreal music promoter Reuben Fogel.

"Most artists don't want to put in that type of commitment. It shows that work pays off. In this business you cannot just rely on the talent of the artist. Celine is a great example of how important it is to have good marketing and total dedication to develop a star."

In 1982 Celine recorded songs in France and Quebec for her third album, *I Have So Much Love For You* (*Tellement J'ai D'Amour Pour Toi*.) Rene was instrumental in choosing the title of this album, which was named after a song written by Eddy Marnay. Nobody at the time realized that Rene was giving a subtle message to his adolescent 14-year-old protégé.

"Rene was adamant on selecting this song as the title of the album," said one of Rene's longtime buddies.

"Many friends thought that he was delivering a message to his wife Anne. But to me it was obvious that it was directed for Celine. He couldn't take his eyes off her and he couldn't outright tell her because it could have caused a scandal and could have cost him his career.

"At this time that Rene was already constantly talking behind his wife's back, and he loved to have the attention of much younger girls because I think he was going through a mid-life crisis," he said.

"But I remember during one of our frequent luncheons together that he asked me if I thought that 14-year-old Celine was sexy. I laughed in his face and I thought he was joking. But he was very serious. I didn't know how to answer him," the friend added.

The biggest test of Celine's young career came at the 1982 Yamaha World Popular Song Festival in Tokyo before a crowd of 12,000 people and 115 million TV viewers. The French version of *I Have So Much Love For You* won a gold medal in the best song category. Celine was also honored with a special Musician Choice prize.

Upon her triumphant return to Quebec from Japan, Celine was publicly congratulated by the Premier of Quebec, Rene Levesque. This started a love affair between Celine and Quebec's politicians. In the coming years, she would frequently be seen dining with Quebec's leading politicians, some of whom (like Levesque) believed that Quebec should secede from Canada, while others were against this Separatist Movement. In general, those in favor of Separatism are French-speaking, while those against it are English-speaking. It was a no-win situation for Celine to get caught up in these politics as each side battled the other - especially because she was starting to break into the English market. But some believed she showed more favor to Separatism and were infuriated.

On the one occasion when she voiced a political

message, she got badly burned. Publicly, she turned down the Felix award (Quebec's Grammy) in 1990 for best English-language singer for a song she sang in English, and her gesture caused a ruckus because it seemed to support the Separatist Movement.

"The public knows I'm still French-speaking, even when I sing in English," Celine explained in refusing the award.

Celine's record label Sony was furious with their star for getting embroiled in a political debate and threatened to dump her from its English roster. Rene took this threat to heart. And, he felt the barbs from the English media, his friends, and prominent Quebecers who were angered. He knew this political hot potato had to be dropped immediately because it could only harm Celine.

"She's young and rebellious like many people her age," Rene said. "Sometimes she doesn't realize what she says. It will never happen again." And, it never did.

Many people close to Celine say that after this incident Rene never permitted Celine to make public statements without his consent. He also forced her to make an emotional plea for Canadian unity when she sang at the World's Fair in Seville, Spain in 1992.

"Even though she made it clear that she was not a separatist, she lost the confidence of many of her Quebec supporters who are in favor of seceding from Canada," said one Montreal journalist. "Those are the people who supported her from day one. But Celine was becoming a big English-language star and couldn't care less about her early fans any more."

Celine won 15 Felix trophies between 1982-85. Her corny hymns to John Paul II during his 1984 Canadian papal visit made Celine the butt of many jokes and parodies for years by Quebec's humorists. From then on, she has been frequently called a country hick, or "ketaine" (kitschy) in Quebec slang.

* * * * *

Since Celine had become a teenage singing sensation, she had been the focus of romantic passions from a lot of young men. Many musicians she worked with tried hard to get her to go out on a date to a movie or a restaurant with them. Celine found a couple of them to be attractive, but things usually never got more serious than a peck on the cheek because of Rene's constant warnings to her about the perils of romance.

"If you want to be a star, you have to pay the price," Rene would constantly drum into her head. "Now's the time for you to just concentrate on singing and nothing else. Boys are a dime a dozen and you'll have them at your feet when you become a big star."

Looking back, many people close to Celine and Rene agree that Rene used this tactic because of his hidden romantic interest for Celine. This would seem to contradict many rumors that he was already sleeping with her.

"Rene's the master planner and he wanted to make sure that Celine stayed available until she reached 18 and then he would be able to make his move," said a close friend of the couple.

"He was always extremely jealous and still is whenever Celine shares a laugh or even a glance with another male. He's always been very possessive of Celine as both an artist and lover because he's so insecure about his age and his looks."

At 16, Celine was becoming increasingly insecure about her looks. She kept her mouth closed to hide an imperfect bite whenever she was photographed. And she was obsessed with keeping her figure extra slim. Celine wanted to avoid winding up heavyset like her mother and would often go days without eating a proper meal.

Her doctors warned her regularly about the perils of anorexia when she was a teenager. Even Celine's brothers and sisters thought that their baby sister looked unhealthy. One of her sisters even once showed her an article about singing star Karen Carpenter, whose life was claimed by a long bout with anorexia.

"You better start eating or you will disappear," her sister warned her. "We don't want you to wind up like Karen Carpenter."

Celine finally agreed to see a dietician who put her on a balanced eating program. But she complained regularly of nausea, weakness and exhaustion during her teenage years, and had many bouts of extreme weight loss.

Celine had her first steady boyfriend when she was 16. He lived next door to her sister Claudette. Rene hoped that the relationship would not get serious because he had developed a romantic obsession with Celine.

Celine and her boyfriend talked about going skiing together and even about having sex. But a two-month European tour away from him put a damper on their relationship. Even though Celine couldn't wait to return to Quebec to resume their romance, she was badly heartbroken upon her return - her boyfriend surprised her by telling her that he had dumped her for another girl.

Celine, in tears, told him, "I'll still wait for you because I love you so much... I'm the one for you. I understand that

I was gone for a long time and you found someone else. But I care for you so much."

"Sorry, but I don't love you," her boyfriend replied. "I need someone more simple and because you're a singer you'll always be gone for a long period of time. I'm also not physically attracted to you anymore."

Celine then went on a huge dating binge. She needed to feel wanted. She dated several musicians, a dancer and even a bartender. But her relationships always wound up ending in the same fashion. She would go off on tour and would be devastated when she returned because her boyfriends fooled around on the side.

"Celine was a hot teenager," remembers one of her ex-boyfriends, who now lives in Montreal. She was very insecure about her looks, so much so that it drove me crazy. I would tell her often how beautiful she was but she didn't listen. She was a nice girl but she seemed screwed up in a lot of ways."

It was at this point that Celine decided to take comfort with an older man, Rene.

"Celine was devastated and thought that she was ugly," said one of her longtime friends. "Rene was there with open arms and helped make her feel good about herself again. I think this is the point that Celine realized she needed a man with experience and maturity. She didn't want to get hurt by a younger guy again. Rene knew all the great lines that every woman likes to hear, and Celine fell for it."

Rumors among their friends were rampant that Celine and Rene were lovers. In public they acted as if their relationship was strictly business but it was obvious to their close friends that more was going on.

"They were always together and didn't look like they just

had a business relationship," said a close friend. "I was not surprised at all when I first learned that they were actually sleeping with each other."

Many people close to the couple suggest that they first became lovers even before Celine became 18. Very few believe Rene's story about how they fell in love when she was 20. A major Montreal tabloid, Photo Police, declared in 1994 that Rene was breaking the law by living with Celine when she was underage. Rene was furious. He launched a $20-million lawsuit, which was settled out of court on August 29, 1997, when the paper retracted the story and made a donation to the Cystic Fibrosis Association of Quebec.

"Rene didn't want to go through with the lawsuit because a lot of witnesses would have brought out a lot of intimate stories - and he knew he could have lost in court," says a reporter close to the story. "His neighbors saw them living together and acting romantic together. And his wife was furious about it all before she finally moved out."

* * * * *

Celine was Quebec's biggest star by the time she was 18. Yet, she threatened to quit the music business repeatedly during her teen years, claiming physical and emotional exhaustion. After her album *Melanie* went platinum (100,000 copies sold) in 1985 and after a gruelling 25-city tour in Quebec, she told Rene that she didn't want to continue.

"It's making me into a complete wreck!" she complained. "I don't have a regular life like the rest of the girls my age. Sometimes I feel like I'm your possession and I have to get up and sing whenever you ask me to."

Rene, who was just as emotionally worn out after going through another divorce, told Celine that he would give her a lot of time if she would listen to his new plan. He wanted to give her career an entire facelift by having her sing in English even though she could barely speak more than a few words.

"We've accomplished everything we can, my dear, in the French market," Rene told Celine. "Now it's time to take a lot of time off and to make you into the mega-worldwide star that you should be."

Thus began Rene's new career as a modern-day Svengali.

At the age of 18, Celine spent the next 18 months transforming herself from a child star into a sexy, English-speaking diva - all under Rene's guidance. She took a Berlitz English course and hired beauty consultants to help her improve her looks. She cut her long black hair which spun almost to her waist and created a halo around her face. She added a touch of strangeness through careful plucking of her eyebrows to give her an air of mystery. She got rid of her girly image, and started to look more like a woman instead of like a young schoolgirl. Rene also sent her to an orthodontist and oral surgeon to perfect her bite. "If you're going to be famous everybody will look at your mouth first," Rene told her. "We'll get your teeth fixed and make you look like a pop princess. "

Celine was often fatigued during her struggle to transform and complained of constant dizziness. One time she vomited on her dentist's lap, almost passing out in his office.

Everybody in the record business agreed with Rene that the only way Celine would break into the world pop stage would be by improving her entire look. Even Rene's mentor Ben Kaye thought Celine had to shed her childlike image.

"In this business sex sells and Celine needed to have an added appeal if she was going to break in the US," Kaye said. "She had too much of an innocent Marie Osmond type look. That image was long out and people were only buying sexy stuff like Madonna."

Rene consulted numerous fashion experts and even took Celine to New York to try on sexy outfits, high heeled shoes and very revealing skirts.

"You look so sexy," Rene constantly told Celine. "You'll turn on the whole house when you sing. You look irresistible - you're a star."

After months of exercising and practicing rock'n roll moves, Celine looked as slim and limber as ever. She had the firm beautiful body of a dancer, with graceful arms, thighs, calves and shoulders. Even her breasts seemed to be fuller than before. When she didn't wear a bra under her dress, her pointed nipples were hard not to notice.

During her English lessons, she developed a sophisticated British accent that surprised many of her friends - especially to the extent where she was starting to sound like Princess Diana. In fact, long before Princess Diana's tragic death, Celine felt a spiritual connection with her and identified with her.

"Celine began to sound like a cross between Princess Diana and a cabbage patch doll," said one of Celine's close friends. "She was trying to pretend that English was her mother tongue but her command of the language was very poor. She'd mispronounce words all the time."

Meanwhile, Rene was busy schmoozing with major record label executives, in hope of landing Celine a major contract. He finally found a big ally in Sony Canada's eastern representative Bill Rotari, who convinced CBS Records President Bob Summers to check out one of Celine's concerts in Montreal. Summers walked away extremely impressed and offered Celine a million-dollar recording contract.

Her first release by Sony, *Incognito*, made her the first Quebec artist ever to go gold in France (500,000 sales). Rene convinced Sony that it was time for Celine to do her English debut album. With the aid of three top producers, David Foster, Christopher Neil and Andy Goldman, Celine launched *Unison* on April 2, 1990. Two singles from the album hit number one on Billboard, and helped launch Celine into a major English player in the music business.

Celine's transformation worked - and she had Rene to thank for it.

Very few critics ever believed that Celine had a shot to conquer the English market when she was younger because she could hardly speak the language. When she heard those remarks, she always responded that Abba couldn't speak a word of English and they became one of the top-selling groups of all time in the 1970s.

The people at Sony were ecstatic and decided to make her one of their biggest stars, next to George Michael and Michael Jackson.

"Rene was the brains behind getting Celine to sing in English," said Ben Kaye. "Nobody believed this gamble would pay off, but once again Rene beat the odds. He took Celine and transformed her entire image into a sexy pop diva. He made all the right moves."

To Celine, Rene became the man who could do no wrong.

5

Rene, the Happy Hustler

It's 11:30 PM and the Golden Nugget Hotel in Las Vegas is filled with gamblers sporting fat cigars, expensive suits, the smell of stale beer and losers' sweat. Rene and his longtime mentor, Ben Kaye, decide to take a break from the blackjack tables and go watch the nightly variety show.

It didn't take long for Kaye to become disgusted with the caliber of comedy that was going on. "These guys are awful," he told Rene as the two of them sipped a couple of Johnny Walkers on the rocks. "I could put these guys under my seat." Rene promptly excused himself to go to the bathroom. Before he returned, the host of the show introduced the next performer.

"Ladies and Gentlemen, from Montreal, the one and only Ben Kaye," the host, clad in a red tuxedo, announced. Rene really did not go to the bathroom. Always a practical joker, Rene went up to the host and convinced him to let his friend Kaye get a shot at trying to make the jam-packed room laugh. Kaye, whose real last name is Kushner, used to work as a comic many years back in Montreal before becoming a manager for several music groups.

Kaye got up and told a few jokes *a la* Jackie Mason, one of his all-time favorite comics, and had the audience in stitches in only a matter of minutes. After his set, he even had a few talent scouts come up and try to sign him.

"I told them to see my manager and I pointed to Rene, who was on the floor laughing," Kaye remembers.

"Rene was always a big joker. But he also knew how to get things done. In a matter of seconds, he managed to get me up on stage in Las Vegas. Millions of comedians would give their left arm for a chance like that! But that's what Rene is like - and that's why he's been so successful over the years. He's not shy to ask for favors."

Kaye, who has known Rene for over 35 years, says that Rene was not in joking moods all the time over the years.

"He went through a lot of tough times and almost wound up on skid row," says Kaye. "But Rene worked hard and always fought for whatever he got. When he first signed Celine and put everything on the line, including his house, to develop her career everybody thought he was nuts. But look at the final result. He certainly is no fool," Kaye added.

Rene Angelil was born in Canada on January 16, 1942, to parents of Syrian descent. His father was a tailor in a factory and his mother Alice was a dedicated housewife. His parents were married for 30 years before his father died.

Rene and his brother Andre grew up in modest surroundings and had been instilled with a hard work ethic by their parents at a young age. A quiet kid who didn't have many friends during his pre-teen years, Rene's parents encouraged him to become a lawyer or an accountant when he grew up.

While attending St. Viateur school in Montreal, Rene broke out of his shell. He met Pierre Labelle and Jean Beaulne and formed a singing group called "Les Baronets." At 19, Rene shocked his parents when he told them that he had decided to quit school and pursue a music career.

Three years later, Rene and his group had become household names in the Quebec music scene.

Rene loved the entertainment scene, and he especially loved being a star himself. He always wore fancy suits, soft Italian boots that shone like mirrors, and usually had a gorgeous, pencil-slim woman a head taller than him on his arm. Sporting long black hair, Rene smiled and preened for the cameras of the Quebec paparazzi, basking in the attention. Beneath the bravado of the young man, the quick, sassy answers about his new found fame, Rene was a whirlwind of nerves and insecurity.

Everything that accompanied the glitz of fame, like alcohol and drugs, almost made him want to quit the business after only three years. The Baronets were doing well, but Rene did not know whether he had a future in the music business. During road trips, he became homesick quickly. Sometimes he dragged his mother on trips because he missed her so much.

All that changed when Rene's group finally found a manager, Ben Kaye. Kaye grew up admiring Elvis Presley's manager Colonel Tom Parker, and he desperately wanted to manage a band. When the Baronets gave him the chance, he turned them into an internationally known act in a matter of months.

"I booked them at local clubs like The Bellevue Casino and the El Morocco," Kaye remembers. "But everything took off when I got them to headline the Steel Pier in Atlantic City and the Caribe Hilton in Puerto Rico."

By 1965, Les Baronets had become Quebec's version of The Beatles. "Those days were the best," Kaye says. "We were always crazy and partied until dawn. There would always be gorgeous women around us when we'd go to

Burnside (now Montreal's famous Ben's Delicatessen) after hours."

In the fall of 1966, Rene married a stunning Quebec woman named Denyse. The couple lived together with Rene's mother in a small house in Laval-des-Rapides, a Montreal suburb. Denyse resented the fact that Rene seemed to prefer the company of his group of fellow deal-makers, most of whom were attracted to gambling. She also could not handle the fact that Rene and his circle of friends were always hanging out with flashy, glamorous women. After only a few years together, she walked out on him . The couple had one child together, a baby boy named Patrick.

Before Rene remarried in 1974, he indulged in the innocent sexual buddings of young girls in Quebec as no one else before him. Les Baronets had become so popular that they had thousands of girls screaming hysterically, moaning and fainting in the aisles at their concerts. It was like mini-Beatlemania, replete with groupies everywhere.

Les Baronets decided to break up in 1973 because they thought they had lost their appeal. Many of their teenage fans were now mothers or approaching 30. Before the band called it quits, Rene met his second wife, Anne, a stunning blonde who was also a budding singer and TV personality. They had two children together, Jean-Pierre and Anne-Marie.

Rene had started a second career as a manager by the time he first met Celine Dion on that famous snowy Montreal day in January 1981. By this time, he had already become instrumental in managing the careers of several well-known Quebec singing stars, including Ginette Reno and Johnny Farago.

Rene had invested almost everything he had in the

career of 200-pound Ginette Reno by the time she shocked him one November day in 1980 by phoning him at his office and firing him. She had become increasingly impatient with Rene's failure to deliver on big promises. She also thought that he was not paying her all the money he owed and once called him to his face a "lying slime."

Rene couldn't believe what Reno did. She had met secretly with another agent and had decided to dump him. He was stunned and shaken. That was one of the reasons why Rene was so optimistic about managing Celine. She was young and didn't know as much about the intricacies of the music business as Reno did, according to his ex-associate.

Celine, the "Home-Wrecking Lolita"

From his first *rendez-vous* with Celine, Rene sensed there was something special between the two of them.

Rene later told his friend, "when Ginette Reno suddenly dumped me I passed the worst Christmas of my life.

"After the holidays, I was in my office staring at all the unpaid bills I had on my desk. In between them was a parcel with a demo tape in it. There was also a message saying 'Listen closely to this cassette.' When I heard it I fell in love with the voice of this 12-year-old girl."

When Celine showed up at Rene's office for the first time with her mother, Rene told her "I'll make you a star within five years."

Rene devoted all his time to Celine and would buy her gifts and take her out to restaurants all the time. This behavior concerned his wife Anne, who couldn't believe that her husband seemed to be falling in love with a "naïve young girl."

Anne, who also worked hard organizing Celine's career during the first few years of Rene's association with her, warned Rene repeatedly that he was playing with fire in the way he charmed young Celine.

"You're supposed to be her manager and you act like you want to get married to her," Anne said during a recording session when Celine was 14 and Rene bought her a bouquet of flowers. "Rene, please wake up. You can get yourself into deep trouble by messing around with a girl that young."

By 1985, Anne was totally fed up, and she and Rene separated because it became clear that Rene was only interested in one female: Celine.

Behind Rene's back, Anne had asked a couple of friends to report to her on his meetings with Celine when she was not present. The reports persuaded her that their marriage was over.

After they divorced, Anne called Celine "a home-wrecking Lolita" and vowed that she would "never talk to that conniving young bitch ever again."

Anne was particularly upset because many people close to the couple warned her that Celine was already secretly sleeping with her husband. And, Celine was hardly 17 then.

"Impossible", Anne would always tell them. "He could go to jail for sleeping with someone so young. I know he likes to look at young girls, but this is ridiculous."

Even Ben Kaye was shocked when he found out about Rene's romantic obsession with young Celine. "He talked to me about it a lot when we'd go out for drinks," Kaye said. "But he said he didn't want too many people to know because he didn't want to be viewed as the Roman Polanski of Quebec."

Inside his large circle of deal-making friends, Rene was treated like a sort of cult figure after he took Celine's career to marvelous heights. But even his friends were concerned that Rene was going a bit too far with his emotions.

"I think it's despicable that Rene hit on his client who's young enough to be in high school," said one of Rene's close friends. "Ever since he did that, I've lost respect for him. I don't even think that he's in love with Celine because whenever he hangs out with his buddies he's always staring at beautiful women."

Rene, the Colonel Parker of Canada

As Celine's career soared, Rene started being referred to as Canada's version of Colonel Tom Parker, Elvis' famous manager.

He harbored no doubts about his motivation for success. He was in it for the money.

"The cars and the houses I've bought I could never afford without the success of Celine's career," he frequently tells his friends. "So the more I buy, the harder I have to work."

However, some of his friends are still not convinced that Rene will be financially set for the rest of his life.

"Rene had money before Celine and he wound up broke," said one old high school friend of his. "Everybody knows that he loves to gamble. He mortgaged his house to bet on Celine's career. One day he might make a similar move and it could backfire."

Rene's gambling has not only been a lingering concern

to his buddies but also to his late mother Alice, who constantly tried to dissuade him from going to casinos. She warned him, always to no avail, that "gamblers never come out ahead." Rene still loves going to the casinos in Las Vegas several times a year. Even a week before he married Celine, he had his bachelor's party in Vegas with several of his buddies, including Guy Cloutier and Ben Kaye.

"We practically had to drag Rene away from the tables," said one of his friends who attended. "He has a lot of money so I don't think it will ever be a big problem for him but sometimes I wonder if Rene is a compulsive gambler."

In the process of making Celine into the biggest female singer in the world, Rene pulled every lever and collected every IOU he had ever earned in the music business. The furies of his ego will never be stilled because he is riding a giant winning streak with Dion that seems to only result in triumph. Although many of his friends and associates perceive him as a "modern day Svengali", he's out there, ignoring any negative comments about him and Celine and constantly making new deals related to Celine's career that bring in even more millions of dollars.

"Let's face it," says well-known Montreal promoter Reuben Fogel. "Without Rene pushing Celine she'd be nowhere. I've seen tons of talented artists over the years go absolutely nowhere because they didn't have the right person out there promoting them."

One of Celine's worst scares happened when she was in jeopardy of losing her voice prior to treatment by a New York doctor. She had major throat problems and came close to losing her voice permanently just before she was to get her big break in the US in 1990.

She and Rene were petrified.

The scare came just as Celine was releasing her debut English album that year. Celine was feeling ill during her long sessions in the studio and thought she had got strep throat. But it didn't go away for months and there were even fears that Celine had throat cancer.

"Everybody was so worried that they immediately expected the worst," said one of Celine's close friends. "Celine said repeatedly that something was terribly wrong with her voice and she afraid that it could be something like cancer. She and Rene were beside themselves with anxiety. I remember how she kept feeling her neck to see if she had any lumps."

Rene first arranged for Celine to meet with a Montreal doctor and to undergo extensive tests. The doctor told Celine that she had polyps on her throat and he recommended surgery. Rene wanted Celine to get a second opinion because vocal chord surgery for a singer is always career threatening. At first, according to one of Celine's band members Rene did not want anybody to breathe a word about Celine's bad health to anybody at Sony Music.

"Rene almost turned blue when he found out that Celine had polyps on her throat," the musician said. "He didn't know what to do because he was afraid that Sony would dump Celine and the whole deal because they might have considered her to be damaged goods."

"It could have been the end of both of their careers."

Rene arranged an appointment with NY throat specialist Gwen Korovin, whose celebrity patients included Frank Sinatra, Cher and Luciano Pavarotti. On their first visit to Korovin's office Celine still barely spoke English and Rene had to translate for her. Celine was so hoarse she could barely speak. Her vocal chords were terribly swollen.

"Please doctor, recommend anything but surgery," Rene pleaded. "Celine is just about to become a star and this could ruin everything."

Rene told Korovin that Celine was as good as Whitney Houston and Barbra Streisand. He then played Korovin a tape of Celine singing and the doctor decided right away that something had to be done to save Celine's voice without surgery.

"Rene was right," Korovin said. "Celine had an incredible voice. I decided to try and save it by putting her on some anti-inflammatory medicine and prescribed a two-week period of complete vocal rest. She was literally not to speak a single word and to use only pen and paper to communicate."

Celine followed Korovin's orders. She sat on a beach in Aruba for complete relaxation, and didn't say a single word. The only way she'd communicate with Rene and her family was through sign language or notes scribbled on pieces of paper.

Korovin's treatment turned out to save Celine's career. Celine fully recovered and managed to avoid an operation that ends most singers' careers.

"Vocal chord surgery for a singer is always a delicate matter," Korovin said. "There is always the risk of scarring and permanent damage. The vocal chords can become stiff and that can negatively affect a singer's range and durability."

Celine remains very grateful to Korovin to this day for saving her career. She sent Korovin a framed photograph of herself after *Falling Into You* sales started to go through the roof.

The photograph had the inscription "Presented to Dr. Gwen Korovin in recognition of your outstanding contribution - 50 MILLION ALBUMS - December 1996."

Korovin said that she considers Celine as one of her dearest friends. "A bond formed between us from that point on," she said. "She became a regular patient of mine and a dear friend. I even attended their wedding, and I get amazing Christmas cards with personal photos from them every year."

Now, Celine imposes Korovin's rules on herself when she's working very hard. She rarely speaks on the day of a concert, always travels with two humidifiers, and does vocal exercises for 35 minutes a day when she's not touring. Often, she gives her voice complete rest by not speaking at all for 24 hours or longer, noted her sister Claudette. Yet she finds a way to communicate with her mom.

"Celine loves to phone our mother every night no matter where she is in the world - even when she's not talking. So, the two of them have developed a special code so they can always communicate. Mom asks her questions, and Celine taps the mouthpiece several times with her finger for 'yes' and once for 'no'. They have whole conversations this way because they really understand each other - it's very touching to see!" Claudette revealed.

6

Academy Awards

Most people in the music industry agree that 1992 was the turning point in Celine's career. With one English and nine French albums behind her, sales of her second English album, *Celine Dion*, immediately soared. Her follow-up to her English debut, *Unison*, became her first gold record in the US, selling well over 500,000 units after only its first few months in record stores.

The first single from the album *If You Asked Me To* was number one on the Billboard charts for three weeks; the second, a bluesy gospel track called *Love Can Move Mountains*, topped the black American charts. Dion was only the second white singer in recent years to crack the black American charts. The other was George Michael's *Faith* album.

Celine finally felt comfortable speaking English and she made her sixth appearance on the Tonight Show with host Jay Leno. She also completed a sold-out tour in Europe, Australia, New Zealand and Japan.

But it was on March 30, 1992, the eve of Celine's 24th birthday, that Celine realized that she was becoming a mega-star. It was the night of the Academy Awards, and Celine and Peabo Bryson performed their winning theme song from the hit movie *Beauty and the Beast* with over two billion people watching on worldwide TV.

Even though their romance began to titillate people surrounding them, Celine and Rene were not yet formally together as a couple. Before they entered the Dorothy Chandler Pavilion that Oscar night, Celine and Rene vowed to keep their hands off each other.

"We've got to be very careful, Cherie," Rene said. "We will be under the watchful eyes of the world and if we even hold hands, they will think that we're having an affair."

Rene still wanted to keep their affair secret because he feared that Celine's male fans would be turned off if they found out that their sex symbol singer was not single.

"A lot of men out there fantasize about being the man in Celine's life because they think she's single," Ben Kaye often told Rene. "You better not disappoint them by announcing you're her man. They might lose interest in her career and stop buying her records."

So when Celine and Rene entered the Academy Awards, they were very careful to avoid giving the hordes of media present any indication that they were romantically linked.

Celine sat nervously with Rene as she stared around the star-filled room. "I can't believe we're here," she whispered to Rene as Sharon Stone got on stage to present an award. "I never thought that we would make it this far." Then she got nervous because it was almost her turn to sing.

"I hope I don't screw up," she said in a very shaky tone. "I'm so nervous I feel like I'm gonna pass out."

"Don't worry," Rene said. "They'll love you. Just pretend it's just another gig."

Celine didn't show any signs of nerves when she sang her duet with Peabo Bryson. But, when she got onstage, she immediately noticed Barbra Streisand sitting in the first row and couldn't believe that she was singing in front of one of her idols.

"Everything was all right when I got onstage," Celine said. "I just closed my eyes and started singing. But when I opened them, I noticed Barbra Streisand in front and that was very intimidating to see her right there."

Casting Celine along with Peabo Bryson was the idea of master showman and producer Vito Loprano. The Canadian Sony executive pulled every connection he had to get Celine to sing the lead song of Disney's *Beauty and the Beast*. It was the only way, Loprano thought, that Celine's worldwide profile could be raised.

"We've got to break her into the U.S. market to get the big bucks," Loprano would often tell Rene. "Maybe the only way to do it is if we get her to sing in a couple of big movies."

Backstage after the show, Celine was mesmerized as she mingled with top Hollywood stars and producers. One director, who didn't know that Celine was not single, invited her to go to a "wild after hours" party with him. He even told Celine that she turned him on and that he thought she was extremely sexy. "You're such a sweetheart," Celine said. "But I'm already going to another Hollywood bash. Maybe another time."

Rene had secured a table for him and Celine strategically placed next to Hollywood's biggest stars at a post Academy Awards party that lasted until the wee hours of the morning. Celine virtually ignored the man she loved sitting to the left of her and couldn't take her eyes off the man sitting to her right, Hollywood star Patrick Swayze.

She introduced herself to Swayze and told him how

much she had always admired him, especially in *Dirty Dancing*. Rene looked uncomfortable and extremely jealous as Celine and Swayze talked.

"I think it was at the Academy Awards that Rene knew that he might have created a monster," said one of his close friends. "After that night, Celine talked for weeks about the gorgeous male stars she met at the awards. Rene realized that he'd have to try to somehow keep Celine more secluded or else he might lose her to some stunning male movie star who was much younger. "Rene was starting to react like Tommy Mottola did with Mariah Carey. Very jealous and possessive," the friend says.

Mottola, president and CEO of Sony Music, played Carey's Svengali at the start of her career and then married her - much like the situation between Celine and Rene.

By the mid 90s it became evident that Celine was rising much faster and farther than Mariah up the pop ladder - and Mariah was to become infuriated and extremely jealous.

According to a Sony insider, shortly before Mariah's break-up with Mottola in the summer of 1997 her anger peaked. She blasted Mottola, saying, "I'm sick and tired of all the attention that you and Sony are giving Celine!

"Why don't you do the same thing for me? I'm your wife!" she roared.

"My career is going down the drain because of Celine!

"I'm not going to play second fiddle to some singer who's nowhere as good as me!" Mariah said.

Interestingly, when she finally left Mottola that summer, she was often photographed with gorgeous young hunks - and she looked happier than ever.

Upon hearing of their breakup, Celine was often questioned by her friends: "Are you next?"

Rene's possessive attitude would cause a lot of tension between Celine and him in the next couple of years. He wouldn't let her leave the house without his consent and he'd ask their household staff to keep a watchful eye over his star while he was away.

"He tries to keep Celine cooped up like a young chicken," said a former member of the couple's household staff. "He tries to make sure that hardly anyone visits Celine and that she never goes out without him. I felt really bad for her because she was losing out on doing things during her youth like nightclubbing and going to movies."

A few weeks after the Academy Awards, Celine felt the impact of what happened at the big event.

"It's the biggest television show and it's very prestigious and the song won and it's a classic and I was part of it," she said excitedly. "I congratulate Anthony Hopkins as he passes me backstage, and then I go onstage and Barbra Streisand is sitting in front watching me. Then, Liza Minnelli goes by and later I'm eating shrimp with Patrick Swayze, and I meet Paul Newman at the elevator. It was too much!"

But a sad part of Celine's rise to stardom is that she rarely gets to mingle with the Hollywood crowd she admires. She's rarely seen at parties, and many insiders ignore her, according to a Hollywood insider.

"One of Celine's problems is that she comes off as a kind of country bumpkin. She's just not one of the in crowd."

7

Too Sexy for Me!

Celine had been a huge Michael Jackson fan since the days of the Jackson Five and _Thriller_. When she attended celebrity masquerades and Halloween parties, she loved to dress up as Jackson himself, replete with a black curly wig and a single glove.

In the spring of 1992 she attended a preview screening of one of his new videos and got up and danced in her seat several inches away from the screen.   "Oh God," Celine squealed as Michael Jackson fondled black supermodel Naomi Campbell. "He's too sexy for me!"

Celine had been enthraled and amazed by Michael Jackson since she was a young girl. She loved to watch him dance and sing, and she believed he was one of the greatest - and sexiest - performers in the world.

Once, after Celine met him and shook hands with him at the Grammy Awards in Los Angeles, she told friends that "Michael is the sexiest man in the world - and he's got great buns!"

She also joked to one friend about how cool it would be if she went on marry Jackson instead of Rene.

"Could you imagine if I became involved with him?" she asked one close friend.

"We have similar physiques and even our bone structure is alike. Our kids would turn out to be so sexy!"

Celine said.

She even admitted she dreamed of him and fantasized about being intimate with him.

"Celine got off on the whole story that Michael harps about all the time, you know, 'poor me, I never had a childhood', because he started singing professionally as a little kid and he never got to do all the stuff the other kids did," her friend says

"She identified with him because it was the same thing for her - she started singing professionally as a little child, and never took all the steps along childhood that 'normal' children do.

"Plus, both she and Michael came under the control of an overbearing older man - in Michael's case it was his dad who was the manager pushing The Jackson Five, and in Celine's case it was Rene.

"All that, along with the fact she found him so physically sexy and such a great performer on stage, turned her on totally. She often talked in a joking way of her desire to have an affair with him - but it didn't sound like a joke to me," the friend said.

As for Jackson, he took an immediate liking to Celine, even asking a Sony rep if he should invite her to his ranch for the weekend.

Jackson said, "she's the type of woman who'd be ideal to start a family with..."

But the rep told him, "don't bother - from what I understand, she's not interested in getting involved."

Jackson wasn't deterred, and decided to make his move on Celine. He sent her the black fedora that he wore on his music video, *Billie Jean,* and it instantly became one of Celine's cherished possessions. But shortly after,

Jackson married Lisa Marie Presley, and gave up his efforts to snag Celine. Yet, Celine never got over her attraction and admiration for him, and it almost led to a major career blunder a couple of years later.

* * * * *

Celine's squeaky clean image got severely tarnished when she participated in a TV special in February 1994 with one of the people she admires the most in the music business, Michael Jackson. It was Jackson's first performance since he agreed to pay some $15 million a month earlier to settle a civil suit alleging that he had sexually abused a 14-year-old boy. Everybody around Celine, including her family, friends and the media was shocked that Celine, who had always been a staunch children's rights activist, would participate in an event organized by a possible pedophile.

But Celine was so thrilled with the prospect of being with him and working with the famous singer that she put all doubts aside.

"From that day on I knew that Celine was a total hypocrite and phony who would do anything to promote herself," said a musician who used to work for her.

"Celine was always posing on magazine covers with sick or underprivileged children and then she agreed to work with a guy who was accused of molesting boys. When I worked with her I always found something phony about her but this was the last straw. She lost my confidence and that of many others around her forever," he said.

Jackson decided to invite Celine to participate in his Las Vegas show after an Epic executive who worked closely with both him and Celine suggested to the eccentric pop star that it would be good marketing to have Celine appear with him.

Look at all the bullshit that's gone on over the last year... you should invite someone who has a positive image with kids to be there," the Epic executive told Jackson.

"Everybody in the world knows how much Celine does for children's charity causes, and since her image is so clean people will think that she doesn't believe the allegations against you," the Epic exec said.

It also didn't hurt to have Celine present because she had the number one song at the time, *The Power Of Love*. The Epic label is affiliated with Sony Records, Celine's recording label.

Even though she was riding the number-one spot herself on the record charts and had begun a sold-out world tour, Celine's people felt that appearing with the much maligned Jackson would only enhance her profile. But the whole show backfired quickly.

The media was very sceptical about the show which took place at the MGM Grand Hotel because it was a "Jackson Family Tribute" paid for and orchestrated by the family itself. Most media thought that Jackson was using the TV special as a desperate attempt to turn around his shady image. Indeed, many people involved with the production of the show claimed they were never paid.

Rene, who had been instrumental in convincing Sony to make Celine a guest star, felt no qualms about having Celine appear with the alleged child abuser.

"Absolutely none," Rene said. "This is show business."

But one member of Celine's band said Rene's only concern was record sales.

"He has no compassion," the band member said.

"If Rene knew that 20 million people would watch a Charles Manson performance, he'd make sure that Celine would be on the card. And besides, the event was in Las Vegas so it gave Rene another excuse to blow some money in the casino."

Celine didn't see anything wrong with performing next to Jackson. When asked later how she felt about participating, she looked like she was in awe of the pop legend. His alleged child abuse did not concern her in the least.

"I didn't even think that he would remember me," she said. "But I did have the number one song, so he may have heard it on the radio."

Although proceeds from the TV special were supposed to go towards helping survivors of the recent Los Angeles earthquake, nobody in the end saw a dime, including Celine.

The show's ratings were a complete bust and Jackson was unable to pay the expenses of many of the crew and performers because of the huge deficit, totalling in the millions of dollars. The whole debacle left a dark cloud over a confounded Celine.

All of Celine's spontaneous acts of generosity towards children, which brought her numerous honors and accolades around the world, were now erased in the eyes of many of her fans.

"Celine should never again be invited to perform for a major children's event," said Alain Charbonneau one of her longtime fans who has followed her career since she was a teenager.

"After she agreed to support and perform with Michael Jackson, she lost all the respect of her fans. It's obvious that she has no principles."

But a long-time friend of Celine, Nathalie, who has known the singer since she was a teenager, says the criticism is unfair.

Celine is one of the most sincere and genuinely good people you'll ever meet," she says passionately.

"One thing about her is that she always believes the best about people. She knows about all the lies which have been printed about her in the tabloids and I think she figures that the accusations against Michael Jackson are in that same category. She loves kids and if she thought he had done those things, she would never have agreed to appear with him. I guarantee it."

8

The "Royal" Wedding

Quebec was in a state of uncertainty in October of 1994. There was the possibility of political turmoil due to an upcoming referendum to separate from Canada. Unemployment figures skyrocketed to their highest level in 15 years. English-speaking people and many businesses continued their mass exodus to more prosperous places and everything seemed to be changing for the worse. While the future of the province seemed bleak, there was one bright star shining through the night: Celine Dion. At the top of the American Billboard chart was her number one single, *The Power of Love*, and the waiflike Quebec chanteuse was now an official mega pop superstar. Before the year ended, Dion's gushing charm and bright smile would be plastered all over the press one more time. But it would have nothing to do with her singing or record sales.

The intercom sounded in Rene Angelil's office. His secretary had finally tracked down Vito Loprano, head of the Sony Music office in Montreal.

"Vito, I've got big news for you," Angelil said. "I'm going to marry Celine and we're going to have the biggest wedding ever in Canada."

Loprano, a teddy-bearish, dark-haired, middle-aged man, paused and then congratulated the manager whose client had made Sony millions of dollars that year.

He told Rene that they should meet with Celine and start making plans for the December wedding. After they finished talking, Loprano called his right hand man Richard Walker into his office and told him the news. His voice filled the Sony Montreal office in a crescendo of anger.

"I don't know how we're going to tell the media and the Sony people in the US about this about Celine marrying her manager! He's 27 years older than her!" he said.

"This is just what we don't need right now!"

Loprano had always been nervous about the couple's relationship, knowing that a lot of people were suspicious about it ever since Angelil had found Dion when she was only 12 years old and brought her to live in his office. Not the least of those suspicious about the arrangement was Angelil's wife who eventually left him after he refused her ultimatum to sever ties with the young Celine.

The Sony image-makers went into a conundrum every time subtle insinuations about the two appeared in the Quebec press and they had gone to great lengths to portray the relationship as strictly business. It wouldn't do to have the image of Quebec's national sweetheart and Sony's upcoming superstar tarnished. It seemed as if all the careful spin-doctoring Sony had been doing was about to blow up in their faces.

Loprano, dean of Montreal's music executives, decided it was time for him and his team to roll up their sleeves and oil up the hype machine. His goal: Put a positive twist to the marriage announcement and restore calm if the media got into a malicious frenzy about the marriage.

Soon after Celine and Rene announced their romance on a popular local TV talk show hosted by a well-known personality, Lise Payette, Loprano called several of his friends in the media and told them the "great news" adding that they'd be "the first to know when it was time to release more specific details about the wedding".

The next day, the newest chapter in the real-life soap opera of the Dion fairytale was splashed across the press. Quebec's biggest newspaper, Le Journal de Montreal, ran a photo of Celine and Rene with a headline in French, "Le Couple Royal" - The Royal Couple. Loprano, Celine and Rene couldn't have been more pleased. Not only was their romance accepted, but none of the reporters berated the couple for lying about their affair for so long.

Loprano had known Rene for years while Rene made his name marketing local artists. They had much in common, or so Rene believed. Both were shy and introverted but, on the inside, they had volcanic-type personalities that could erupt at any moment. For a decade, their career paths tracked one another closely. Rene was constantly trying to get Loprano to sign Montreal talent and Loprano always refused politely.

Loprano has a reputation for inspiring fear. His tantrums are legendary. After Rene announced his plans to marry Celine, Loprano gave his staff a warning not to release any details whatsoever, and not even to talk to anybody about the couple's romance or wedding - or else they would be fired.

Rene's quest was complete. He had managed to put the clinching hold around his fair maiden and the pop world had its fairytale. But by any standards it was an unusual romance. He himself could not have imagined that he would marry the girl whom he met twelve years earlier, when she showed up at his office with a demo tape and began singing into a pen off his desk, pretending it was a microphone.

Rene was overwhelmed by Celine's presence and the control she had of her young and powerful voice. He immediately invited her to live in his office. This would start the wreckage of Rene's second marriage to a stunning blonde singer, Anne, who was 12 years younger than him. Rene soon began spending all his time with Celine and reports were rife by the time she was only 15 that they were having an affair. Anne was furious at Celine because Rene mortgaged their house to pay for the production of Celine's first two albums. Then, she picked up clue after clue that the young girl she invited into her home was stealing her husband's heart.

When she finally threw up her hands and filed for divorce, Anne called Celine a "home-wrecking Lolita."

"From day one, Rene was like a modern-day Svengali," says a close friend of Rene's. "He shaped her every move, to the point where he organized oral plastic surgery for her to make her look more like the international femme fatale she has finally become."

It was not until she was 16 that Celine was given permission to call Angelil by his first name, even though rumors abounded that they were already romantically involved. After Rene would tuck Celine into bed around 10 PM, he would go party at discos with his close set of friends. Rene was a keen wine drinker and was known as a regular on Montreal's trendy Crescent and St. Denis Streets. Celine didn't smoke and never drank, preferring to spend her free time listening to Barbra Streisand and Michael Jackson albums and watching TV. Even in her wildest dreams back then, she couldn't have known that these great heroes of hers would one day be tracking her down to perform with them.

* * * * *

Rene had flogged his own music wagon up the mountain himself as a singer and then saw his fortune plummet down into the valley when he had a dispute with a couple of fellow band members about the direction their group should take. Unable to compromise, Rene left the band, and, needing work, started his own talent management and promotion firm. He became involved in the careers of several local acts including singer Ginette Reno. Rene was hitting on all local stars to sign with him, but none of them had the potential to become an international star like Celine.

Understanding the saga of the relationship between Rene and Celine is essential to understanding Celine's rise to stardom. Celine worked hard to develop her voice, sometimes practicing in front of the bathroom mirror for as long as six hours. She studiously listened to her voice teacher and to Rene with complete devotion and never tried to be the center of attention. Rene was crazy about his priority client. The fact that Celine loved domesticity to the point where she would often iron his shirts and perform other household duties made Rene feel even more affectionate towards her.

The gifted Dion lofted Rene to new heights as her career soared. Many doors that had been closed to him for years were now open, including that of well-known Montreal pop impresario Donald Tarlton (Donald K. Donald). Rene's associate Ben Kaye was good friends with Tarlton and convinced him to put Celine on several top showcases. Tarlton also helped get Celine a gig to sing the national anthem at the Olympic Stadium before Montreal Expos baseball games. Rene didn't have to line up anymore to get into popular downtown nightclubs like Thursday's or Winnie's. When club bouncers saw him they immediately greeted him at the front of the line and let him in.

"Rene kept their love affair really low-key because he was afraid of getting into trouble with the authorities," said the friend. "He also feared that Celine would be criticized for stealing another woman's husband and that a scandal would wreck her career."

All this time, however, Celine's parents gave their full blessing to the odd-ball relationship.

Celine's mom, Therese, said, "Rene's the best man for my daughter - so why shouldn't they be a couple. It doesn't matter that he's 27 years older - he's a wonderful man."

They finally decided to go public with their affair in 1992, largely because of a massive life-threatening heart attack Rene had suffered earlier in LA. He had suddenly begun complaining of unbearable chest pains, and Celine bundled him into a taxi and rushed him to Emergency at Mount Sinai Hospital. She was petrified that Rene might die right there. She said later the experience made her realize she wouldn't be able to hide her love for him in public any longer. Doctors found that his heart problems were caused by blocked arteries, which they treated with drugs and a new diet. When they told Celine there was a glimmer of hope for him, she promised Rene that if he pulled through they must go public with their love affair and get married.

While he recuperated in hospital, Celine made her first big decision without Rene's guidance. She decided to fly alone to New York and then to Europe to continue her promotional tour without him. On the plane, she cried the whole way. "I'm doing this because Rene would want me to,"

Celine told her family. "I have to get used to being on my own. Rene won't be around forever." Later, she told an interviewer that, without Rene, she felt "like a car without an engine... he's the engine of my life, and, without him there are things I simply can't figure out."

Disturbingly, Celine had a premonition of Rene's medical emergency. It happened while she was staying with her parents one weekend a couple of months before going to LA. When one of her sisters politely asked about Rene's health her reply startled the assembled company. She found herself saying that she felt Rene "was going to drop if he wasn't more careful..."

Celine and Rene returned to Quebec in September on a bleak Wednesday afternoon, and during the drive to their Laval home, they formally discussed an issue which had troubled them for many months - whether or not they should sign a prenuptial agreement. Rene convinced Celine that they would be together "forever" and they didn't have to sign any sort of business contract. He told her she was free to leave him at any time if she became dissatisfied.

"Celine's career was reaching international heights and this was the perfect time for Rene to put a stranglehold on her whole career," said Tom Williamson, a former associate of Angelil. "Rene was worried that his prized possession might get turned loose with his bad health and all, so he put Celine on a sympathy trip and it worked. He got total control of her life."

But as the public celebrated their engagement, Celine's world closed inexorably around her. There were many tears in the months leading up to the big day and many more to come after that. It was during this turbulent time that the rumors about Celine's anorexia began. Both the American and Canadian tabloids had a field day. What they didn't know then was that Celine had fought the anorexia battle even as a teenager, and the problem never seems to end.

Since her teens, Celine's weight went up and down like a yoyo. This time, her waist shrank down to 22 inches after the engagement was announced, although she managed to get it back up to look good for her wedding. But she had to work hard to gain the weight, and she needed the help of a strict dietician. While she was thin, she became very self-conscious and wouldn't expose her taut belly as she liked to because her ribs looked like they were painfully sticking out. She was also concerned about her health, and complained about sometimes missing two periods in a row - saying that this certainly wasn't helping her become pregnant.

When Celine was literally skin and bone during the late 80s, she thought she was fat. Now she realized that she might be sick. Meanwhile, Rene had weight concerns of his own. His belly was getting big again and he was concerned that he wouldn't be able to fit into his tux for the wedding. He even once joked that people would think "I'm pregnant before I'm even married." He enrolled in a weight-watchers program and went on a strict diet of fruit juice, vegetables, whole wheat bread and a pasta or rice dish for supper.

During this time some ill feeling between Rene and the Dion family boiled over into a series of vicious exchanges.

There were constant battles between the Dion family and Rene about how the wedding should proceed. Celine's mother, Therese, wanted her daughter to be wed in their hometown, Charlemagne. Several of Celine's siblings even threatened to boycott the wedding if it was not in Charlemagne. But Rene insisted that it was important to make a giant royal show of it, and that the international celebrities he was inviting would come only to a big city like Montreal. Rene won in the end, but his arguments backfired when not a single famous American celebrity attended.

Another dispute involved the fact that Rene wanted his own children to play a more prominent role in the proceedings. He thought they were being ignored because of Celine's large family. The strain on both families became very intense and, understandably, Celine found it impossible to concentrate on her music career. She decided to call a meeting of her whole family. She convinced her 13 brothers and sisters to go along with Rene's plan, and they finally acquiesced.

Indeed, a big challenge involved the Catholic Church. A controversy developed about the question as to whether the Church would sanction the marriage, since Rene was already divorced twice. One Montreal tabloid said a Papal dispensation would probably be required. To top it off, this particular church, the Notre Dame Basilica, was one of the grandest and most well-known in the world. Not only would the couple be flaunting the normal Catholic rules, but they'd be doing it in the most public way possible. As always, Rene's will prevailed and the controversy died as suddenly as it began...

* * * * *

Celine awoke early on the morning of December 17, 1994, unusual for her because she has a habit of sleeping until the early hours of the afternoon. She was in a suite on the 29th floor of Montreal's posh Westin Hotel. It was the start of what she later described as "the most hectic day of my life." She turned on the TV in her room and the second news item she saw concerned the crowds starting to gather outside Notre Dame Basilica to line up for her wedding later that day. She began to feel a deathly dread combined with great anticipation at the event which lay ahead.

Several of Celine's sisters, her makeup artist, and her dressmaker, Mirella Gentile, were on hand to make sure that the bride stayed calm and looked her best. Celine was a bundle of nerves but tried to calm down in the days leading up to the wedding by getting facial and massage treatments. She and her mom also went for a nude whirlpool bath the day before the wedding at Montreal's exclusive Le Sanctuaire health club.

"I couldn't believe it," said one member of the club. "A day before Celine's wedding she showed up in our whirlpool and came in naked along with her mother! They were pleasant and Celine was cracking jokes. But she looked nervous and a bit stressed out."

Her brother Paul remembers his sister's transformation when he saw her in her wedding gown. "She looked amazing in the gown and with her makeup. I never saw her look more beautiful."

Her father, Adhemar, who was to give her away, was thrilled. "You look so beautiful, my favorite girl," he said as they walked to the elevator from Celine's private suite. Even after their marriage and to this day, Celine and Rene continue to sleep in separate rooms. Rene liked his privacy and usually got up very early. His loud snoring also made him self-conscious about sleeping with Celine. One time after they made love, Rene fell asleep right away and started snoring so loudly that a concerned Celine suggested that he go for acupuncture treatment the next day.

* * * * *

Celine climbed into the white Rolls Royce limousine with her father with several practical considerations to overcome. Her dressmaker realized too late that they had not taken the size of the limo into consideration when they had designed the ivory silk wedding gown with its 20-foot long embroidered train. In spite of all Celine's effort, it was badly crushed during the short journey to Notre Dame Cathedral.

When they reached the Basilica, surrounded by a fleet of police escort cars, they could hear the crowd cheering. Police had closed off the streets of Old Montreal that afternoon, allowing Celine's adoring fans to line the streets to catch of glimpse of the procession. As she got out of the limo, her fans, who had braved frigid temperatures and a snowstorm, held its collective breath in awe. Adhemar leaned heavily on Celine as they walked up the steps of the Cathedral. The crowd cheered wildly when Celine waved to them. One young fan yelled out "Celine, our Cinderella!" Another, only a few feet from the bride, tossed a bouquet of roses towards her. The cavalcade of stargazers seemed to distract the bride. Directly behind Celine was her sister Ghislaine and her niece Audrey, the flower girl. Celine made sure that she was surrounded by them in order to avoid contact with her worshippers.

As she entered the church, Celine was left standing at the inner door of the Basilica in full view of all the guests because her train was too long to fit in the lobby and still close the door leading to the aisle. She kept standing there in full view of everyone as her makeup team descended on her to do a final touch up - which took a total of 20 minutes.

It was a bride's nightmare. Instead of making a single grand entrance, guests in all the pews turned and stared at her over and over. Celine told her makeup artist that, "this is so embarrassing, we should have come earlier so the whole room wouldn't have to see me being made up!" But Rene had been counting on making a lot of money by selling their private wedding photos and video to their fans, so the makeup had to be perfect for the production. So Celine demurely stood there, at the back end of the aisle, for a full 20 minutes.

Rene had already arrived a few minutes earlier, accompanied by his son Patrick and his daughter Anne-Marie. One fan yelled out that handsome Patrick looked like he should have been the groom instead of Rene. Patrick became the butt of jokes amongst his friends after Celine and Rene announced their wedding plans. They all had a common theme - the age difference between his father and Celine. Celine had to adjust to cross-currents within the family. While she enjoyed an amicable association with Patrick, her relationship with Anne-Marie and with Rene's mother, Alice, were polite at best.

The Angelil women were cordial to her face but behind her back Anne-Marie called Celine a "witch" and said that Rene's mother didn't think the relationship would last more than three years.

Rene waved to the crowd repeatedly before entering the church. More than 500 guests had already arrived including a slew of local celebrities, such as comedian Anthony Kavanagh, popular talk show host Sonia Benezra and the unpopular former Prime Minister Brian Mulroney with his wife Mila, who were greeted with a resounding loud chorus of boos by the crowd. The crowd seemed very disappointed that not one of the Hollywood stars who had been invited showed up. Celine had invited many of her celebrity acquaintances including Jay Leno (on whose show she had announced her wedding in the US), Mariah Carey and Michael Bolton, but none of them came.

Another no-show was Celine's longtime musical collaborator Eddy Marnay, who told the media he couldn't fly in from Paris because of his handicapped son. But he told friends he never intended to go because he felt he had been pushed aside. "I was with Celine from the beginning - but since she broke into the English market and made it big I've never been given the credit due me," he said.

The only famous people the crowd got to see were has-been local celebrities, like singers Rene Simard and Mario Pelchat.

The giant church, which has a capacity of 3,000, was practically empty - yet no uninvited guests were permitted in. Celine's huge team of security guards made sure that they remained outside in the cold. When one uninvited guest tried to pretend he was part of the procession, he was quickly escorted into a police car and driven to a local precinct. No charges were filed but he wound up watching highlights of the wedding on TV in a police holding cell.

After the 20 embarrassing minutes of having her make-up redone before walking down the aisle, Celine's eight bridesmaids, all her sisters, took hold of her train and got ready to march to the altar. They wore dowdy hooded monk-like cream colored dresses which hung loosely from their shoulders like used tablecloths. Celine, with her father leaning heavily on her arm, walked with careful slowness down the blue-carpeted aisle. Celine had plenty of time to spot the guests and she nodded to members of the

Canadian Sony entourage in the front rows.

She kissed her father tenderly on the cheek as Rene came to take her to the ornately decorated altar. Rene stared at her for about ten seconds before taking his bride's right arm. He could see through her veil the pouty bee-stung lips, cascading honey-brown hair and deep brown eyes that often make Celine resemble a waiflike supermodel.

Celine cried once during the Catholic ceremony and borrowed a tissue from her father. Rene, who sported a braided pigtail of grey hair, beamed the whole time and didn't show any signs of nervousness. The couple had sold the exclusive photo and video rights for $ 200,000-plus to the Quebec magazine 7 Jours, so they barred all other photographers (and fans) from attending. However, unknown to her heavy security team, the US tabloid The Globe had managed to sneak in three undercover photographers, one of whom would be physically ejected during the wedding reception.

As Rene put the wedding ring on her finger, Celine curtsied and flashed her familiar smile to all the guests to show off the big diamond. There were only a few moments of fun and spontaneity during the dreadfully solemn proceedings. Celine's bottled-up sparkle became evident when the renowned Montreal Jubilation Gospel Choir sang *Glory Train* and she seemed to come alive. She clapped her hands in the air above her head, as if she was encouraging the guests to get up and clap and dance with the choir. But they had become so intimidated by all the security apparatus that nobody moved an inch.

"We all felt like we were at a Royal Wedding," Ted Tevan, a Montreal talk show host who knew Angelil and

Kaye, told his radio listeners. "We were all overwhelmed by the security guards and the press outside the church. TV crews from everywhere were following this event."

And newspaper columnist Nathalie Petrowski of La Presse said she couldn't get over how sad Celine looked on her wedding day. She later wrote, "in Celine's own words, this was the greatest show of her life. Not an event, not a ceremony, not a human experience : *a show*. This is all Celine and Rene know about - how to put on a show."

The guests were escorted to chartered buses to take them back to the Westin for the wedding reception. They all had to go through another tight security check before entering the hotel. Even Celine's immediate family members were searched. When one of her sisters said, "you don't have to check me, I'm Celine's sister, a security guard grabbed her and told her, "you're not going in unless I check you."

After going through security, the guests passed through a thick black curtain to a heavily guarded lounge where a long waiting game began. They were served finger food and booze as they cooled their heels for several hours. Meanwhile, Celine and Rene held a 20-minute press conference. Rene was very quiet, but Celine joked with the media and showed her youthful exuberance. She told the press that, "we plan to practice a lot to produce a baby. We want to have children, but I don't know yet if I'll be able to."

Her young, fun side was revealed for a few seconds here and there in front of the reporters. Once, she pretended she was swooning like Scarlet O'Hara, and she gazed upwards adorably, placing one hand on her forehead and the other on her bosom as she dipped far backwards.

Then, the couple disappeared for another two hours to

continue shooting their video, leaving their guests cooling their heels and complaining about the long, tiresome delays.

Finally, Celine and Rene made their grand entrance at 8:30 PM to form a reception line at the lounge. As Celine bent over to kiss an older woman who was sitting down, her left breast popped right out of her low-cut dress - and she didn't even notice.

One male guest asked another - "did you see that?" - while the other nodded with a big smile, answering, "I sure did!" A photographer pointed out to Celine that her nipple was showing. Celine laughed and quickly re-adjusted her dress and kept on greeting guests.

Some of the guests got so fed up that they abandoned the reception and went home by the time the sit-down dinner began at 10 PM, more than five hours after the ceremony had ended. The Perry Carmen band played some classic standards as the crowd began dancing. One youngster noticed NHL star Patrick Roy on the dance floor and interrupted him for an autograph. The first big moment of the night came when Celine stood in the middle of the dance floor, twirling around and around in a circle as her dress spread out - making her look like a magnificent dancing swan. She was surrounded by her 13 brothers and sisters - all older - who serenaded her with a song they had written especially for her. After the song, she hugged her siblings and they all wept tears of joy.

The hours went by and the ballroom started to empty. Eventually, at 2 AM, an eight-foot-tall cone shaped wedding cake studded with pastry cream puffs and topped with flowers was wheeled out. Celine and Rene cut the cake, took a few nibbles for the camera, and the cake-eating ceremony was done.

At about 3 AM, an adjoining room was opened to reveal a gambling casino using fake money, and many of the remaining guests wandered over from sheer boredom. Even Rene hung out alone at a gambling table, shooting dice with Celine nowhere in sight. Rene, a passionate gambler, came up with the idea to have a casino at the wedding. "It's the tackiest idea I've ever seen at a wedding," remarked one guest.

* * * * *

The couple had been claiming that their grandiose wedding was costing $500,000, but hotel employees and catering staff laughed when they heard that figure. One Westin insider said, "for instance, the five-course dinner would normally cost about $75 per person; the alcohol, another $75. But the hotel reduced the rate to less than half that because it wanted the free publicity. And a lot of other freebies were provided by her 'honored' suppliers.

"So it cost less than $100 per person, for a total of less than $50,000 for the 500 guests. Even with the elaborate winter castle sets and the formal string orchestra during dinner the total cost couldn't have been more than $100,000 - so the $500,000 they claimed was totally nuts!"

Even worse, the employee added, "Celine and Rene totally stiffed the hotel staff. No tips were given to the food service staff - and they were royally pissed off.

"Then, I saw one bellboy take five loads of wedding presents up and down the elevators for Celine - and he didn't even get a $1 tip. All the other stars who come here like The Rolling Stones and Madonna were very generous and friendly. But not Celine and Rene. It's all a lot of hype."

9

After the Honeymoon

During their very brief honeymoon, Celine and Rene spent hours in their gigantic oval hot tub sipping champagne and cold, dry white wine while they lay naked and made love in the soothing water. They'd even nap with their heads propped against the side, and end up with their skin looking like wrinkled prunes.

They reaffirmed the deep bonds which held them together. Their marriage gave them an entry into the mainstream of the establishment of society and wealth which would not have been possible on the same level had they kept their love affair hush and remained single. But they still could not move in their own inner circle, the world of Hollywood celebrities, without whispered, back-stabbing comments and insults.

Rene quickly discovered that Celine was more sexually active than his two previous wives. She always was horny and would make sexual gestures at Rene endlessly, he told his friends - half bragging, half complaining. If Rene was too tired to make love, Celine would rub his back for an hour until he purred with relaxation. Then she'd go into the kitchen and prepare Rene a huge meal and put it on a huge tray and bring it out, sometimes wearing only panties and a bra. She then settled Rene among the cushions on their bed and made sure he ate well to gain some energy for an evening of lovemaking.

When singer and friend Michael Bolton first heard that Celine and Rene were tying the knot, he reacted in disbelief. "He's almost old enough to be her grandfather," Bolton told a band member. "Not that I have anything against either of them, but I wouldn't bet on their marriage lasting very long."

Bolton knew the couple well because he had booked Celine as his opening act a couple of years earlier on his world tour. He caught on quickly that the couple were involved when one of his musicians hit on Celine backstage before a concert and was quickly scolded by Rene.

"Please don't chat up Celine, she's got work to do," Rene firmly told him. "I'm not chatting her up, we're just talking so leave us alone," the musician quickly replied. Rene had a look of disgust across his face and looked like he was about to explode.

Rene, not knowing what to do next, told the musician that if he didn't stop chatting up Celine that he'd make sure that Bolton would reprimand him. Unaware that Bolton was just a few yards and privy to the entire heated exchange, Rene then went as far as saying that he would get Bolton to fire him if he didn't back off.

Bolton, like the all-American he is, jumped into the fray and told Rene in no uncertain terms to back off and stop trying to curtail the freedom of speech of his band members.

Bolton told Rene, "everybody's free to do whatever they want in my band. I'm not going to be a policeman. If you have a problem with somebody it's between you and them. Leave my name out of it."

Rene was shocked. Seconds later, he reacted by dragging an embarrassed Celine back into her dressing room. Everybody on the stage, including Bolton, broke out in guffaws of laughter.

"Who the hell does that fat idiot think he is?" asked one member of Bolton's band.

"He acts as if he owns Celine!"

* * * * *

Rene, characteristically, barely stopped working during the honeymoon. In fact, he had Celine so tightly booked that she even had to interrupt their honeymoon to take a quick flight to London to appear on the TV show Top of the Pops to sing *Think Twice*.

But more annoying than the heavy work schedule was the triggering factor that led to a trial separation - Rene's obsession with talking on the phone. It led to many, many arguments between the newlyweds.

One night when Rene simply would not stop talking, Celine became increasingly dismayed. She had complained to friends that, "Rene's more interested in talking to his buddies on the phone than enjoying the private moments away from friends and business that most newlyweds cherish!"

This night, she became totally fed up.

"Rene, you've been on the phone all night!" Celine said angrily. "I don't mind a couple of calls here and there but it seems as though you're more interested in finding out about how your friends are keeping rather than spending time with your wife!"

Rene quickly apologized and admitted he was wrong. To make it up to her, he decided to take Celine out for a huge champagne dinner the next day.

"Put on your best dress, Cherie," he said. "We're going

out on the town for the best dinner you can imagine."

Celine quickly forgot about their squabble and went out with Rene till 4 AM. She felt great. But as the days went on, she became increasingly concerned because he went right back to his same old phone habits. She started to feel like the second fiddle to the people Rene constantly called.

The final straw for Celine came a few months later when Rene got back on his cell phone once again at dinner after he had promised not to.

Celine hit the ceiling. Uncharacteristically, she put her foot down and gave Rene an ultimatum.

According to a friend, she demanded a one-month trial separation during her upcoming Australian tour.

"When I come back, if you don't stop talking on your cellular all the time I'm going to leave you for good," she told Rene adamantly.

"While I'm gone, make up your mind. I'm tired of hearing you talk on the phone from six in the morning until we go to sleep. Sometimes I feel as if you would prefer being married to your cell phone instead of me!" Celine said.

The couple was separated for more than a month. Rene gave friends the excuse that he was decreasing his touring with Celine because doctors warned him that a grueling touring schedule might aggravate his serious heart condition.

When Celine returned from Australia, Rene immediately told her that he'd only talk on the phone during office hours and that he promised not to even touch a phone or dialpad during the evening.

"All my attention after work will be focused on you, Cherie," Rene told a relieved Celine. "I won't even bring my cellular when we go to restaurants to make sure I don't get tempted to pick up calls."

Celine was a bit surprised that she had won even one victory over Rene, and she seemed to enjoy having an upper hand for awhile...

-- PHOTOS --

MILESTONES
in the lives of
Celine and Rene

Celine and Rene wed on December 17,1994.

Celine and her fiance raised a lot of eyebrows.

Celine and Rene, last Montreal press
conference, December 17,1996.

The author gets an autograph from Celine for
a young friend, while Rene looks on.

The author interviews Ben Kaye, longtime associate of Rene Angelil.

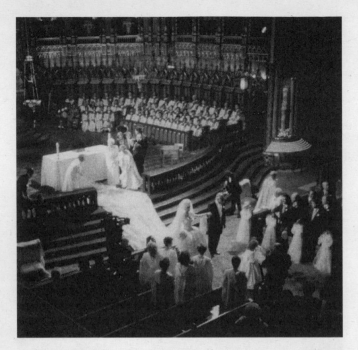

The "Royal" Couple likes to say the wedding
cost $500,000, but an insider pegs it at less
than $100,000. This photo was taken by
a very unauthorized photographer.

Celine leaves her
mother-in-law's funeral,
May 29,1997.
She and Rene had a
heavy falling out on the
way to the church.

Celine shows her youthful exuberance a few months before her wedding.

Celine with her team and Sony execs. She worked hard to boost her strength and weight for this press conference at the end of 1996.

10

Anger, Jealousy, and Suicide Threats

Less than a year after their wedding, Celine and Rene's marriage started to faltcr, and there were acts of violence and anger.

A major sore point was the fact that Rene was becoming increasingly jealous of Celine's friendships with younger men - and he sometimes became violent when they'd return home from a day in the studio. According to friends, he'd throw household objects like lamps around their home and threaten to hit her.

On one occasion, after a heated argument, he grabbed a full vase of flowers and threw it right out the window to their backyard.

Rene was convinced that Celine enjoyed being a rock star more than being his wife. He started to resent her ambitions and retaliated with several late-night outs with his male friends while Celine remained at home under the watchful eyes of the couple's household staff.

"Rene started to realize that the age difference between himself and Celine was too much," said an ex-housekeeper of the couple.

"When young business associates came over to the house for drinks, some of them would stare at Celine in awe because she could be very beautiful and charming during her better moments. Rene thought some of these guys were attempting to hit on Celine, and it made him furious. You should have seen Rene's face as he tried to contain his anger!

"Then, after the men left, he'd go ballistic. He'd often accuse Celine of flirting with them and encouraging these guys to come on to her. No matter how much she denied it, he'd keep ranting and raving at her. Finally, they'd grow tired of the screaming and go to bed angry.

"These marital wars were taking a toll on both of them, and something was bound to happen," the housekeeper said.

Celine soon found it impossible to continue pretending to her family and friends that her marriage was sound. She couldn't carry on as if nothing had happened between her and Rene. Even though her latest album, *D'Eux*, produced by Jean-Jacques Goldman, was smashing the French record market, she had never been unhappier in her personal life.

Her family grew increasingly concerned about Celine's faltering marriage but they didn't want to butt in. Her mother Therese told her daughter repeatedly to try to work things out. But her mother was also making lots of money selling her by-now famous meat pies "Les Petits Pates de Maman Dion" and she didn't want to offend Rene, who was instrumental in helping her market the pies and in giving her advice on how to run her business.

"I don't know what I'm going to do," Celine told one of her close female friends. "Rene is just so jealous of any man that I even say hello to. He's becoming so paranoid that it's wrecking our marriage."

She had to summon all her emotional strength to keep their West Palm Beach house at peace. Her own impulse was to crawl into a quiet room and just let desolation wash over her. But she couldn't permit herself to do that forever.

After one of Rene's blowups – sparked when he caught Celine talking to her Montreal pal Barry Garber on the phone – the couple exchanged vicious words and both became so angry they absolutely ignored each other for an entire a week.

"I told you that I don't want you talking to Barry," Rene warned Celine. "He's a great guy but I think he has a huge crush on you and you don't seem to mind. You're always flirting with the people we do business with. Stop it!"

After Celine screamed back at him to get off her case, the silent treatment began... the two of them would sit on their striped canvas deck chairs on the terrace of their home, with their backs turned to the sea, and not say a single word to each other.

Celine has a gift of reposeful silence and she found it easy not to ask Rene what he was thinking. She couldn't believe the worm of obsessive envy that ate at Rene.

"It's obvious that he's jealous that I'm the star of the show," Celine told one member of her backup band. "He gets so upset when any man even looks at me. Maybe Rene hopes that I will start breaking out in pimples and get fat so that men won't look at me!"

Long hours of introspection when Rene left Celine alone in their mansion forced Celine to begin second guessing her decision to marry him. But, as always, her guilt lingered, the guilt she knew she had no reason to feel.

"Even though Rene gets so jealous, he's still responsible for all my success," Celine would tell close friends. "I can't just throw out so many years of hard work together. I must try to patch things up."

One late night, looking wan and depressed, Celine

waited up for Rene to come home from a night out with his "buddies", because she was planning to try to patch things up.

But hour after hour rolled by without his return, and she began to stew. By the time he finally showed up at 4 AM, Celine was furious. At first she let out her anger, yelling at him at the top of her lungs. She issued an ultimatum to her husband - shape up or ship out, and then tried to reason with him as calmly as she could.

"Rene, things can't continue this way," she said pleadingly.

"I don't know what I've ever done to you but you seem to want to hurt me. I love you but if you continue to try to bring me down and to cut me off from the rest of the world, I will go back to Quebec and live with my parents. I've had enough!" Celine said.

Rene tried to be rational and gentle to calm her down, but her emotions couldn't be reached by logic.

"I'm sorry if I upset you, my love," Rene told Celine gently. "But you always overreact about little things. Every couple has ups and downs. Don't worry, things will work out. You don't have to go back and live with your family... I'll make sure everything's perfect again..."

For the next few weeks, the tension between Celine and Rene simmered. They were preparing to go to France to attend the world's most prestigious music conference, Midem. Celine threw herself into a schedule of activities so full that her energy was totally consumed. At the end of the day, she would be too tired to quarrel with Rene, who was also busy making arrangements for concert tours and TV appearances.

But a few days before leaving for Midem, Celine and

Rene once more had a huge blowout after she criticized him for not making a more serious attempt to have kids. "I'll decide when and where we start our family," he told Celine.

"From now on, you should just worry about singing. Let me worry about what goes on in the bedroom!" Rene said angrily.

This infuriated Celine and drove her into a deep depression. She had wanted children desperately, and she had told this to him and to the whole world - even on their marriage day - and he always acted as if he was in total agreement. But now it looked to her like that was a sham.

According to an ex-member of their household staff, Celine stopped eating and was on the verge of self-destruction. In the next few days, Celine paid only passing attention to Rene. She felt that she was getting no respect from him, despite the past 15 years of dedicating her life to him. To her, Rene's respect was always a thousand times more important to her than any amount of affection or money he could provide her with - and now it seemed as if it was all thrown out the window.

"Celine looked worse than I had ever seen her and Rene didn't seem to mind," said the former staff member. "I felt so bad for the poor thing and I wanted to tell her to leave him but I couldn't because I needed the job..."

Around this time, the staff member came upon a very unusual scene.

"I walked into the den as I was cleaning up, and I clearly saw Rene sitting on the couch watching a video of himself and Celine in the nude making love! They were totally naked on the TV - and I said, 'what's that?' in my surprise," she said.

"As soon as Rene noticed me there he shut off the TV

video.

"He had made a video of himself and Celine making love in their bedroom. I don't think that Celine even knows about it!" the staff member said.

A couple of days later, Celine decided to do something about her unhappiness. According to the staff member, while Rene was watching an afternoon hockey game featuring The Colorado Avalanche – a team run by his longtime buddy Pierre Lacroix, Celine went to the garage of their Florida home, got into her BMW, and turned the ignition on. She left the garage door closed and spent close to 15 minutes breathing in the exhaust and carbon monoxide. Aware that Rene did not know what she was doing, Celine honked a few times to try to get her husband's attention.

In other heated moments during past arguments, Celine had threatened to commit suicide several times.

And, in 1990, she described a disturbing, recurring dream she had six nights in a row: She was on the roof-top ledge of a highrise with police cruisers and ambulances swirling far below her at street level. In the dream, as a cop approached her and closed in to grab her, Celine jumped and felt herself falling through the air. On all six nights, she awoke just before she was about to hit the ground...

Rene never took her suicide threats seriously because she seemed to be talking only out of anger.

Now, upon hearing the honking from the garage, Rene left the hockey game, jumped off the sofa in their living room and rushed to the scene.

In a thick haze of smoke, he found Celine at the wheel of her car, looking drowsy and almost unconscious. Rene immediately grabbed the keys out of the ignition and half-carried and pulled her out of the smoke-filled garage. There was smoke on their faces and on their clothes, and the whole house stunk of the exhaust as he brought her onto a couch in the living room.

Rene was furious, and after waiting a few minutes for her to begin breathing normally, he asked Celine what she was doing.

"I just feel like going away for a long time," she told him. "I'm so tired off all the bullshit between us, Rene. I don't want to fight with you anymore."

Rene, also looking extremely worn out and exhausted, went to the kitchen and brought her a glass of orange juice. He wanted to take Celine to the hospital, but she convinced him not to. They knew the tabloids would go nuts over a story about an attempted suicide by the world's reigning diva - and that Sony executives would probably freak out, so they decided to keep mum about what had transpired. Celine also promised that she'd never do anything like that again...

But years earlier, she almost ended up killing herself and a friend during another crisis. This incident happened while she was driving her girlfriend through the scenic Laurentian Mountains in a new Jeep Cherokee. It was just before she hit the big time with her first English album, and she was exasperated about her painstaking struggles to become a star, saying she felt like "a battered rag doll."

Celine's friend says, "Celine was behind the wheel when she had a panic attack and began yelling, 'I can't take it! I can't take this shit anymore!' - and she began steering over to the edge of the road towards the mountainside, and a 100-foot drop. I panicked. I grabbed her hands and the steering wheel and took control of the car right away, and yelled at her to slam on the brakes. After the car stopped, we switched places and I drove the rest of the way to

Celine's parents' home. We never spoke of the incident again - and even Rene doesn't know about it..."

Whatever secrets Celine and Rene had together about their difficulties, they kept to themselves. The secrets somehow seemed to strengthen the bond between them, but it had nothing to do with love and everything to do with destroying both their reputations.

Even when their family members and close friends enquired about tension between the couple, they'd invent some lie that was plausible enough for everyone to believe.

"They would always cover up the marital problems with some disgusting lie," the staff member said.

"When Celine tried to commit suicide in the garage, they really decided not to breathe a word of it. I know it happened because I was outside on the patio watering flowers when I heard the commotion in the house - so I peeked in and saw Rene carrying a practically unconscious Celine in from the garage area. The house and garage smelled terribly of the car exhaust fumes for days later, but neither Celine nor Rene ever mentioned a word about it."

Divorce Talk

At Midem, Celine was a huge hit. Out of the hundreds of artists present, Celine definitely attracted the most media attention. But before the conference was over, the first public scandal of their young marriage erupted.

A reporter from the glitzy French tabloid Voici overheard Celine talking about getting divorced when she was having coffee with a friend in the Carlton Hotel in Cannes. The next day the magazine ran a huge story insinuating that Celine would shortly leave Rene because "Rene was in no rush to have kids and it was tormenting their marriage."

A media storm broke out. Tabloids around the world had a field day. Even Quebec's most reputable newspaper, Le Devoir, ran a story about Celine's troubled marriage.

Rene was furious when he found out that Celine talked in public about their marriage. In their hotel room, he tried to pick up a mini fridge to toss out the window. He was beside himself. He was also concerned that Sony would be nervous because their new, expensive *Falling Into You* album was due to be released in a few months. He was petrified that Sony might pull the plug on the project.

A couple of days later, a Monday, Celine issued a public statement in a desperate attempt to deflect the rumors about her troubled marriage.

"I want to say I'm crazy about my husband Rene," she said. "I love my husband, who's also my agent, more than anything. C'est mon coeur, c'est mon tout."

This statement was orchestrated by Rene and Celine's team of publicists. Once again, the couple managed to turn a grim situation around quickly and convince the public that nothing was wrong in their relationship.

"It's amazing how they manipulate the media!" the former staff member said.

"I was there and I know that their marriage was on the rocks and almost over. But when the media and then the public finally got wind of it, Celine and Rene killed the news.

"Instead of trying to work things out, they got together and put all their energy into releasing a statement to convince everybody that nothing was wrong.

"Rene was more worried about his and Celine's careers than he was about her affection towards him!"

11

Controlling the Media

Celine is getting ready for an interview with LA-based writer Sara Scribner of US magazine. Scribner was warned by the editor of the Hollywood star-filled magazine that Dion does not like getting asked questions about whether or not Rene is infertile or about the huge age difference between her and Rene.

Scribner was told that those were the conditions of the interview and if she didn't like them, she would have no story.

"I'm looking forward to interviewing Celine Dion," Scribner told her editor before heading off for the interview. "But I'll ask her whatever I want."

Scribner watches as Celine sits in a black barber chair wearing only a white bathrobe, waiting for the photographer to enter the well-known SmashBox photo studio in LA. Celine's getting ready for a gruelling ten-hour session of posing for the US Magazine feature on her. She cracks a joke to Rene in front of a couple of the studio's staff.

"Hey Rene," Celine says with a huge smile, "maybe we can make our baby right here. Wouldn't that be something? Our baby would destined to be a star!"

Everybody present in the studio, including Rene, bursts into laughter.

Before the photographer arrives, Scribner asked Celine

if she has a weight problem. Rene jumps out of his chair a few yards away and interjects.

"Look, if could you please stick to questions that are pertinent to Celine's career," Rene tells a surprised Scribner.

"Otherwise I'll have to cut short the interview!"

Indeed, Rene wasn't kidding. He has cut short or prevented many interviews of Celine. He looks at an interview with the press as if it were a gift that Celine was bestowing upon a reporter.

Scribner wasn't very happy about this turn of events, but she did the best she could to get her story - and she didn't bring up the weight problem again.

In the process of trying to protect their reputations, Celine and Rene pull every lever to make sure that their media coverage consists of self-aggrandizing comments - almost as if their own PR agent wrote the stories.

They threaten editors, reporters and photographers as part of their gargantuan efforts to manipulate and control any and all press coverage about Celine.

Their manipulations border on the paranoid.

If Rene gets wind that somebody wants to write something that he hasn't approved of, he gets into huge fights with the reporter or the editor concerned. Sometimes his attacks are limited to verbal scares, but he doesn't mind going to any lengths to suppress a story. In fact, he's even bribed reporters with money to back off.

When Rene found out in October of 1996 that Quebecor, a major publishing firm, had commissioned writer Nathalie Jean to do an unauthorized biography of Celine, Rene freaked. He got into his car and sped to the downtown Montreal offices of his lawyers Kaufman-Laramee.

"No matter what, we've got to stop publication of this book!" he told the firm's senior lawyer Steven Shein.

"I want you to contact the writer and do what you have to do to stop it."

Nathalie Jean's book was scheduled to come out in the spring of 1997. Rene wanted her to defer publication for several years so as to not cut into sales of Celine's own authorized biography scheduled to be published by Christmas of 1997. Celine hired her own PR agent's husband, Georges-Hebert Germain, to write it.

In the end, Rene worked out a deal with Jean not to publish her book for at least three years, paying her off with a reported $ 35,000. As part of the deal, Quebecor was promised a piece of the action of the authorized autobiography, perhaps by being the distributor.

Jean said that her book promoted Celine more than anything else and that she was surprised that Rene was so determined to gag her.

"Everything about it is above board," she said. "There is nothing explosive or shocking in the book but I guess they didn't want me to cut into sales of their book by Germain. I still want to publish my manuscript, but not before three years."

Rene was proud of his triumph over Jean.

"It shows that money talks," he told Celine.

"Who would have thought that I would be able to shut up Quebecor, one of the biggest publishing houses in the world?"

Unlike many American stars who are happy to be in the limelight regardless of the type of coverage, Rene has the old-fashioned, condescending belief that the public must be spoon-fed a fairytale type of reality - and he instilled that concept into Celine.

To maintain their media fairytale, they sometimes use blackmail.

For example, Montreal photographers are told that if they sell photos of Celine to undesirable tabloids, they'll never be invited to any of her press conferences or shows again.

One photographer who earns a fair amount of money selling Celine photos was so paranoid about angering Celine that he refused to sell a plain exterior photo of her house to a magazine because she hadn't given her permission!

Celine's managers even bully large magazines, such as TV Guide of Canada. Early in 1997, the magazine hired well-known Canadian writer Rosa Harris-Adler to do a cover article on Celine following the American Music Awards. Harris-Adler was granted a 15-minute phone interview - but even before she had a chance to type a single word, Celine's managers freaked out.

They came to the strange conclusion that her questions were too aggressive and they phoned up the TV Guide editor within hours. They gave him this ultimatum: drop the writer immediately, or Celine and Sony would never cooperate with the magazine again on articles involving their stars.

"TV Guide did cave in immediately and fired me from the project," says Harris-Adler. "It was crazy how the Celine group acted. They were totally paranoid."

"Actually, I really liked Celine and was going to write a nice feature about her. I have no idea how they developed the weird concept that I was going to criticize her. I've never seen anything so ridiculous," she added.

The editor not only acquiesced, but bent over backwards to appease them - he promised to give Celine a second cover spread, and to place a free ad for her Cystic Fibrosis Association fund in an upcoming issue! Only then did he breathe a sigh of relief.

Sony Music was a big advertiser in TV Guide's record of the month club ad inserts. TV Guide was worried that they could potentially lose millions of dollars in ads just because of a measly dispute with Celine. The magazine made sure that at the end of the day, Celine walked away very happy.

In another case of their bullying, Sony provided photos of Celine to Chatelaine Magazine of Canada to use for a cover - and then complained to the magazine after publication because they didn't like the photo the editor had picked.

When the editor protested that she used a photo given to her by Sony, Sony execs said that was no excuse. They tried to bully the magazine into doing a second cover to "make up" for not using the best photo - but in this case, the editor refused.

One strange case   involves the publication of this book, Celine Dion: Behind the Fairytale. A major Paris-based publisher wanted to translate the book into the French language for sales in France and Quebec, but backed down at the last minute. They said they were nervous that Sony would retaliate by harming their CD-sales division!

The paranoia of Celine and Rene spills over onto her family members. They have been instructed in no uncertain terms not to talk to the media or else risk losing their privileges - such as their $100,000 Christmas gift plus other favors she grants them!

One of Celine's brothers declined to be interviewed for this book. He did admit, however, that he never talks publicly about Celine because he fears losing his position as head manager at Nickels restaurant, a chain owned by Celine and Rene.

"Why would I talk to a member of the media?" he said over the phone. "If I tell you something bad, I could risk losing a very good situation that I'm in because of my sister's success. I can't say anything that would risk getting me cut off."

12

Celine's Breakdown after the Atlanta Olympics

In the months leading up to the Olympics, Celine's marriage had actually started to crumble. Celine, usually upbeat and protective of Rene, occasionally blasted her husband in front of others with verbal barrages, which he absorbed in silence. When Rene suggested during a rehearsal for a show after the Atlanta Games that one of the backup musicians was playing too loud, Celine quickly jumped on Rene. "You do your job and we'll do ours," Celine snapped at Rene. "Why don't you go for a long walk outside and let us rehearse in peace. Let's just get the job done. If we want your musical input, we'll ask for it." Rene, without answering back a single word, got up and returned to their home.

A close friend of Celine says she was thrilled when she heard about the incident. "This is what she must do to become her own person. She has to stand up to the monster in her life. He has controlled her and manipulated her most of her life. Hopefully, she's finally realized it and wants to break away."

When Celine finally got together again with Rene after the rehearsal, he confronted Celine and told her he wanted to apologize. "I've been under a lot of pressure because we have to finish our tour and I'm still confirming the final details for our European tour in a couple of months," he said.

"I've been worried about you, Cherie, because you seem to always be nervous. I hope I'm not the cause of this."

Celine started to cry and she hugged her uncharacteristically placid husband. She told him that she reacted hastily and she felt bad in recent weeks because she was directing her anger and stress at him.

"I'm so sorry, Rene," Celine said. "These past few months have been so demanding on both of us. I'm so happy you opened up your feelings to me. Sometimes I find it hard to even talk to you because we're both so busy. You know how bad I want to start a family and it seems that because of work, we'll never have time to start one."

Once again, Rene assured Celine that when the tour wound up in six months their number one priority would be to have kids. "You know when people work so hard it's impossible to make kids even if they try," Rene said. "I'm not infertile or anything like that. It's just our minds are so preoccupied now that it's impossible to even attempt to have kids. But after the tour we'll take a year off to start a family. I promise you."

Celine was elated that Rene finally committed to starting a family together. She always thought in the back of her mind that it was easier for him to delay having children with her because he had already three kids from his previous marriages. Rene's commitment to starting a family was a blessed reprieve for her. She felt as though she could now concentrate on finishing the tour, eagerly awaiting a long overdue vacation that would give her and Rene the chance to get make her pregnant. Even though she felt tired, she gave Rene her full commitment on what was arguably her greatest professional challenge. And she infused her spirit with optimism for her life and career.

With the challenge of the Olympics coming up, Celine and Rene bonded together tightly as a winning team and put everything else aside, as they always did over professional matters.

Celine's new healthfulness lasted only until shortly after the Olympics. During a concert in Tinley Park, Illinois she almost did not make it to the stage after a performance by her opening act, the Irish group The Corrs. She felt tired and run-down and moments after The Corrs left the stage, she almost collapsed to the backstage floor with what one observer described as "a near complete nervous breakdown."

There was chaos backstage as Rene dragged Celine into the wings and slapped her face hard.

"Get up, Celine!" Rene pleaded, as several members of crew of backup musicians and stagehands surrounded them. "Get up!."

Celine regained consciousness, and, within five minutes, she was on stage dressed in a snappy white pant suit belting out *I'm Your Lady*. After making a few comments about her recent Olympics experience, she got the whole crowd in the New World Music Theatre tapping their feet to *Seduces Me*.

Everyone was deeply relieved that she was able to rouse herself together and perform, but it was clear that it could happen again.

Over the next few weeks, Celine continued to feel terrible. As the tour progressed, her lack of energy was becoming a debilitating problem. The only thing she could attribute it to was the gruelling work of combining performing and being a housewife to Rene.

"Even when they tour Celine makes sure that all of Rene's shirts are properly ironed and that his clothes are clean," says Rene's close friend and associate Ben Kaye.

"Celine's a throwback to the old days because she grew up in a family of so many children. No matter how tired she was on the road, she'd still make time for all the things an ideal housewife does. That's the type of girl that Celine is."

As worried as Celine was about the way she felt, that wasn't her most gnawing concern. She was terrified that her looks were deteriorating and that her fans would no longer find her attractive. She had already received bad reviews for altering her appearance before the start of the tour. She dyed her hair blonder and coiffed it differently, which many thought made her look ten years older.

"Once, when Celine looked in the mirror she didn't recognize herself," says a close friend of Dion's.

"Many of us thought that she changed her hairstyle to look older because so many people were saying that Rene was too old for her - and that they looked more like father and daughter instead of husband and wife.

"Rene loved the fact that Celine was able to look less youthful. He never liked the criticisms and comments about their age difference. Now people were not so taken aback anymore when they saw the couple together in public. Celine didn't look almost thirty years Rene's junior anymore. She started to look about only ten to fifteen years younger, but her fans didn't like it," the friend said.

As the 1996 show caravan plodded through the States at the end of the summer, Celine became increasingly ill.

One week before the start of her European tour in the fall, Celine was forced to cancel five sell-out shows in the US and Europe. She told Rene that she felt as "if she was about to die."

Rene immediately called Dr. Sydney Neimark, a specialist in gastroenteritis who had looked after Celine before. Neimark ordered that Celine check into a West Palm Beach Hospital to undergo extensive tests. He also ordered Rene to cancel the first couple of concerts in Monaco. Rene was furious. He tried to convince Dr. Neimark that it would probably be better for Celine to perform because it would take her mind off things.

"If Celine performs before we give her a clean bill of health, she might be in danger," Neimark told Rene.

"Please think of the well-being of your wife before anything else. She looks terrible now. We must find out how seriously ill she actually might be before we even consider letting her out of here."

After Dr. Neimark finally convinced Rene to cancel the Monaco shows, Rene issued a statement to the press through Murielle Blondeau, one of Celine's press agents. Rene cited chest and abdominal pains as the reason that Celine had to withdraw from the shows. He also assured Celine's fans that the rest of the tour would go on as scheduled.

In order to avoid being bombarded by reporters at the hospital, Dr. Neimark also issued a statement to the media. He said that Celine was suffering from "extreme fatigue as the result of a long and tiring tour."

"Rest, diet and medication have already resulted in significant improvements in Celine's symptoms," Dr. Neimark said. "Celine has spasms in her esophagus – the tube that propels food to the stomach from the throat."

While it's true that Celine has had this problem for many years - often brought on by stress - this time her associates believed it was far more serious.

Celine's friends immediately became concerned that the reports of Celine's anorexia were true. At five feet eight and weighing around 100 pounds, Dion was far below the normal weight for women of that height.

"This had nothing to do with Celine's anorexia," explains one member of Dion's touring crew. "It was obvious to everybody that Celine was going through big personal stress during this moment. She could not handle all pressure that goes along with being famous.

"I know for sure that she briefly considered suicide. She told one member of our crew not to be surprised if does something like jumping off a bridge after one of the last US shows.

"She said that she could no longer go out night after night and entertain people the way she used to. She also said that her private life with Rene was collapsing rapidly. She admitted that she was taking stimulants and anti-depressants."

Even people at Sony were becoming concerned that Celine might not pull through. One Sony insider told The Vancouver Province newspaper that, "everyone who is close to Celine is very concerned about her health and state of mind," he said. "We think she's lost so much weight because of the pressure she is under to achieve success.

"She pushes herself to follow the kind of punishing work schedule that would finish anybody off. Celine has been like that since the age of 12. Her only ambition, and that of her husband Rene, has been to become the best woman singer in the world.

"She has never been able to enjoy the carefree years of childhood or do things young people do. Rene molded her into the woman she is today – she is his creation and she is completely dependent on him. It's an abnormal situation."

Though she felt weak, Celine was determined to continue on European tour. Everybody close to her was worried sick about her fragile state. She spoke to her anxious mother Therese daily as well as to her siblings who were also very concerned. Her sister Manon even encouraged her to give up her singing career until she fully recovered. Everybody was worried that Celine was on the verge of another emotional breakdown.

The cancellation of the Monaco shows gave Celine a three-week break between her US and European tours. In fact, this break was the longest one Celine had taken in years, even longer than her honeymoon or the days before her wedding.

"Sometimes I feel so weak," she told her very worried mother when she returned to her Florida home after doctors ordered her to get lots of rest and eat three hearty meals a day.

"The other day I woke up and could barely walk. I thought I was dying. Maybe it's because of all of the excitement of the past few months. But I feel so good to be back home and to rest. Rene has been very understanding. He makes sure I get really good meals and he has bought me flowers almost every day. He told me to take my time to get better and if necessary, he'd cancel more of the upcoming shows."

Celine then warned her mom not to believe a word of the "stupid" stories that some of the US and Quebec tabloids had been running about her since they found out she was ill. The big tabloids like The Globe and Montreal's French-language celebrity ("vedettes") newspapers had taken notice of Celine's increasingly skeletal appearance and said that she was anorexic. The papers ran shocking photos of Celine, showing her sunken cheeks, her collarbone sticking out, and her painfully skinny limbs. Her entire family, friends and business associates were worried that the anorexia that plagued her for a couple of years when she was a teenager was coming back.

"I assure you, mom, that I feel fine," she told a concerned Therese. "I admit that I have felt nauseous for a while and that I found it difficult to take in food but that was all because of stress and my busy work schedule. This hiatus has given me the opportunity to get myself together. I'm eating well and my strength will come back shortly. I'm starting to feel like the Celine of old again."

During the preceding months, Celine sometimes almost stopped eating. She knew that the eyes of the world would be focused on her and she wanted to have a supermodel type figure.

"I think Celine was way too cautious about her diet," says a member of Dion's touring crew. "Rene had her working so hard for such a long time that sometimes made her too tired to even look at food. She would just go back to her hotel room and conk out. She was too tired to even flap her jaws. Let's face it, Celine was never a heavyweight and people don't judge singers like Celine on how slim they are. They're mostly concerned with how she sounds.

"Even if Celine ate a lot, she would probably not even be five pounds heavier than she is today. I felt really bad for her because when she cancelled all those shows I had never seen Celine look worse. She had a monster hit album out called *Falling Into You*, and if she didn't start taking care of herself it looked like the sequel would be called *'Falling*

Apart," said the crew member.

For the first few days during her rest period in September of 1996, Celine's bones continued to ache and she felt frequently nauseated. Sometimes she slept up to eighteen hours a day during this ordeal in a dark room in their Florida home. Rene was always nearby. While Celine rested in her bedroom, Rene sat in the downstairs livingroom watching TV and talking to business associates on his cellular phone. He would also screen all incoming calls to Celine and only give her messages from close friends or family.

One night when Rene went upstairs to check on his wife, he could barely recognize her. She looked frail and exhausted. This was the final straw for Rene. Despite the possibility of making millions of dollars on their upcoming tour, it was not worth it at the expense of Celine's health. Earlier in the day, Rene spoke to Dr. Neimark who expressed strong reservations about Celine's ability to do the European tour. "I'm telling you, Rene," Dr. Neimark warned. "If Celine goes out on tour, it could damage her health more and it could even cause permanent damage. You better think very carefully before you make your final decision."

Upon viewing a drowsy Celine, Rene clutched her and said, "it's all my fault because I've been working you way too hard. I'm going to cancel the whole European tour in the morning, because I don't want your health to get worse. I just want you to get better, my love, please, get better."

After hearing Rene's comforting words, an exhausted Celine broke down and cried. She told Rene not to blame himself or anybody else. And she made him promise to wait a few days before making any more concert cancellations.

"Rene, I love you so much," she said as tears streamed down her face. "Please don't make any decisions until I get more rest. Give me a few more days. If I don't feel better then you can consider cancelling more shows."

Rene gave his word to Celine that he'd wait a few more days. He kissed his wife goodnight and went back downstairs to watch The Tonight Show. Rene is a huge Tonight Show fan and rarely missed it, even before Celine started singing on it years earlier when Johnny Carson was still the host.

With a nervous tic in his neck and shoulders, Rene took out his electronic pocket organizer to get out Ben Kaye's phone number. He called his longtime mentor and told him how sick Celine looked. He asked him for advice.

"With the album selling so big and the whole world wanting to see Celine, it would be a shame if she couldn't do the shows," Kaye said. "Who cares what those fancy doctors think? If I listened to what my doctors told me, I'd probably be dead by now. Give her a few days rest and try to get her back on her feet. It took you so many years to get where you are now. You can't blow this opportunity,"

Ben Kaye's advice made Rene think twice about making any hasty cancellations. He decided to wait until the last minute to see if Celine was up to going out on tour.

During her recovery period, Celine was virtually cut off from the outside world. Rene made sure that nobody interfered with her sleep and she barely watched TV or read. She just lay there in a deep sleep. Rene or one of the household's kitchen staff would bring Celine her meals on a huge tray. Usually, Rene put a bouquet of flowers on the tray. Celine only put on her white bathrobe to get out of bed to brush her teeth or to stare out the window to get an idea

127

of what the day's weather was like.

Even though her days in bed doing nothing made Celine almost feel like "quitting the music business" there was a deep part of her that needed to be back on the stage. She knew that this was a golden opportunity that she and Rene had worked so hard to reach. While she lay helplessly in bed she couldn't stop thinking about how she didn't want to blow it.

Rene was convinced that Celine was too weak to resume touring. He had already had discussions with the people at Sony about plans to reschedule the tour for the spring and about what excuses they would use to calm the media. But a couple of days later, with a surprise rush of adrenaline that filled her with energy, Celine got out of bed and started singing in front of the mirror like she did when she was five or six years old. Then she started dancing. Rene could hear the din of Celine from downstairs. He went to Celine's room and saw her belting out *All By Myself*.

"You're supposed to be in bed," he told her. "What's going on, my love?"

"Bed is for old people," Celine responded. She then astonished Rene by saying, "I hope you've told the musicians and crew to have their bags packed for Europe because I don't want to be singing there without a band. I want to be great again, Rene. Let's put the show back on the road."

This was the best news that Rene could have wished for. Millions of dollars were at stake. And he also feared that if Celine was ill, Sony would make one of their other artists a priority ahead of Celine. For the next couple of weeks, Celine surprised everybody around her with her renewed vigor and tenacity. She ate lots of meat, vegetables and salads. She also indulged in fancy deserts and ice creams.

Rene was ecstatic. He showered Celine with gifts and clothes and made sure none of his staff or musicians said or did anything to annoy his wife. He warned Celine's musicians and crew that they would be fired if they did anything out of line. When the European tour started a couple of weeks later, Celine looked reborn.

"That's typical Celine for you," said one member of Celine's backup band. "She always works her butt off to bounce back from hard times and adversity. Even when she will be on her deathbed, I won't count her out until she stops breathing."

13

Doctor on Call

The European Tour of 1996 finally got under way and Celine dazzled. Her longing for rest to cure her aching body and her desire to spend more time with her husband became secondary to singing her heart out for hundreds of thousands people from London to Copenhagen. Once again, Celine was able to muster her resolve and assume her role as the world-class performer that she is. Celine seemed to have made a miraculous recovery. But her doctors monitored her every move, and she called them virtually every day because they weren't fully convinced that Rene made the right decision to let Celine continue working.

"If you so much as feel even a bit sick, you must stop the tour immediately," Dr. Neimark warned her repeatedly during their daily checkup chats.

"If you get more sick, it could affect your ability to get pregnant in the long run. Please be wise."

Celine would respond assuringly with, "I feel super - don't worry. I just needed that three-week rest. I feel as good I as I did ten years ago when I sang and did public appearances all day. Everything is fine. I'll finish the tour and then Rene and I will start planning to have a baby."

Celine vaunted her "new energy" by singing with more emotion than ever. Only a few weeks earlier she was on the verge of a big breakdown, according to several people in her camp. They said that Celine was filled then with overwhelming self-pity, grim sulking and melodramatic bouts of loneliness.

"It's amazing, it was only recently that Celine seemed to be at the point of burnout and self-destruction," said one friend. "She looked so bad, almost to the point of being driven over the edge."

The three weeks' rest she had taken seemed to do wonders for her. The European critics gave her more acclaim than ever. Celine, once again, did what she had done so many times before during personal crisis: bounce back.

After several mega shows in France, Celine's tour rolled into Germany. Earlier, German critics found Celine to be "far too commercial and superficial". But this time the Germans fell in love with her. They treated her with the same respect they had previously bestowed on American contemporary rock stars like Michael Jackson, Barbra Streisand and Michael Bolton. One night several hundred people stood outside of Celine's Hamburg hotel chanting, "we want Celine, we want Celine!"

The Frankfurt Daily compared Celine to Elvis, saying, "if Elvis could have witnessed this, he would have been proud of the lady in white who so admirably demonstrated his lascivious hip-swinging and stance with legs wide apart. Celine has charisma, personality and wit."

And, after 6,000 people packed a Hamburg Arena to see Celine, The Hamburg Daily wrote that Celine is a "songstress with a wide range." In Berlin, The Berliner Hopo called Celine "Canada's most successful export item...the Barbra Streisand of the 90s. Her irrepressible joy of life never seems artificial."

The tour couldn't have been more successful - but it began to get grueling as Celine and company continued to roll across Europe. In Denmark, the critics said "time has made Celine a superstar of the kind you thought passed away with Sammy Davis and Dean Martin." The Swiss newspaper, Tagblatt der Stadt Zurich said after Celine's sold-out concert that, "Celine is an elf-like figure with legs like a gazelle, a dream vision...She is the ambassador of love and 12,000 Swiss were very willing to be seduced by her."

Even as Celine felt the great emotional highs from all the rave reviews, she still grappled with romantic problems with Rene. The couple rarely slept together during this tour and when Rene did plop himself down on Celine's bed late at night, he could barely move.

Celine, who always made sure to wear expensive, lacy, sexy lingerie for Rene, would repeatedly try to coax her husband into making love.

Celine complained to her friends that Rene would say, "now's not the time... I want you to relax cause you need all of your energy for your shows. We'll have plenty of time to make love after the tour. I hope you understand, my love."

Celine grabbed on tightly to every word Rene said and was slightly confused about why her relationship with her husband was becoming platonic. But Rene's explanations usually comforted her and made her believe that she was still the center of his romantic universe. He'd also crack jokes about their sex life to make fun of the situation.

"Don't worry, my love," he told her one night in Germany at their hotel after a show, "if you can live without sex for just a few more weeks, I promise you that we'll resume our sex life and you'll be changing diapers this time next year!"

Rene was very busy during this tour making sure there were no glitches. Europe's music critics had been tough on Celine during previous tours and he wanted to make sure that she only received favorable reviews this time. He was concerned about Celine's health and he felt that if she received bad reviews, it could upset her and make her more ill. When they visited cities he verified that the only reviews that Celine read were favorable. He monitored all the newspapers that she would read and even the TV shows that she would watch in her hotel in case of any undesirable messages.

"Rene was terribly concerned about Celine's health and state of mind," said one member of the Dion touring crew. "If a newspaper so much as uttered one unfavorable word about Celine, he would make sure that she would never read it. He knew that anything negative could have had a devastating affect on her because it wasn't long ago that her state of mind was very fragile and worn down. Rene took total control of any contact with the outside world that Celine had."

After Zurich, Celine had a few days off before beginning several shows in England. Rene took Celine on several huge shopping binges on London's Oxford Street and at the world-renowned Harrods, where she ran up a bill for thousands of pounds in less than ninety minutes. This was the typical way that Rene gushed his thanks at her during successful tours. The sky was the limit. Rene would encourage Celine to buy dozens of pairs of shoes, more of her favorite sexy lingerie, skin tight pants and anything else that stimulated her.

Celine hurried around London making TV and radio appearances and going to autograph sessions to promote the British leg of her tour. Wisely, Rene made sure that her four-night stint at London's Wembley Arena was at the tail end of her British tour so that she could use her other shows around Britain as a warmup before encountering London's infamous tabloid press. These tabs, which have a reputation for making and breaking many a rock star's career, turned into pussycats for her.

Before arriving at Wembley on November 16, Celine had already become the toast of Britain. She was being dubbed by the British press as the "songstress of the 90's." Her concert in Manchester two days earlier led a rock reviewer for The Bolton Evening News to write: "Celine's voice soared and teased me like nothing heard before...How such a small frame can boast a voice like that is beyond me."

All four shows at Wembley were completely sold out, a feat usually reserved for Britain's own pop stars like Elton John, Eric Clapton and George Michael. Before her first show, she told The London Evening Standard that before this tour she was frightened of England.

"I'm very, very happy to be returning to London," she said. "But this was not always the case. I used to be frightened of England because I couldn't speak the language. It was like a trauma for me. Now that I'm familiar with London, everything is fine."

Celine did what very few artists managed to achieve: conquer Wembley. British fans, who up to this point had only gobbled up slightly over half a million copies of Celine's *Falling Into You* (well behind the US and Canada), became engulfed with CelineMania. She was an instant hero to most people who attended the Wembley shows. And she also managed to silence the usually sceptical London press.

"Ninety minutes after she first stepped out on stage, and two encores later," gushed London's Daily Star, " the cheering Wembley crowd were still begging for more."

The prestigious London Times wrote: "By the end of the evening, the reason for her success was obvious. Celine Dion is a born entertainer who never met a microphone she didn't like."

Luckily, Celine made it through the European tour with no more difficulties with her health except for the normal wear and tear rock stars encounter during the course of touring.

Her career was building up to an ever-increasing crescendo and she seemed to be the happiest woman in the world. She was also excited about returning to Montreal to celebrate her second wedding anniversary and to spend Christmas with her family.

Still, Celine's romantic problems with Rene kept mounting as the pair rarely shared the same bed or made love.

To add further fuel to the fire, a US tabloid reported that Celine was showing a lot of interest in another man - Barry Garber, the whizkid employee of Celine's main concert promoter Donald K. Donald Productions. Garber already had a reputation for escorting several of Quebec's top female stars, including well-known talk show host Sonia Benezra.

When Rene found out that Garber was hanging out a lot with Celine while he was conducting business meetings, he became enraged.

On a previous occasion, he had confronted Celine and Garber while they were dining together without him. And, he had heard whispers in the tabloids about the two of them being closerthanthis, but he refused to believe them. Both

Celine and Garber continued to deny any romance between them, explaining that they were merely confidants.

During one meeting, Garber told Rene, "come on, Rene, you've got to be kidding - I'd never chase another man's wife, especially yours!"

This time, Rene's jealousy exploded and he phoned Garber personally and warned him to stay away from Celine. Rene was well aware of Garber's penchant for indiscreet dalliances with several well-known Quebec starlets and he wanted to make sure Garber finally got the message to stay away from his wife.

Celine told a friend, "I value my relationship with Barry so much because he's one of the few people I can open up my true feelings to... he's always there to listen to me, always there for me when I need him - unlike Rene who's just too preoccupied with business all the time."

Another close friend explained, "everything was going so smoothly during the tour, and then Rene went berserk hearing that Garber was spending lots of time around Celine. After Rene called Barry and gave him a warning we didn't see Barry hanging around Celine or her entourage for several months."

14

Romance Rekindled: Infertility Blues

Before returning to Montreal from the successful European tour in 1996, Celine and Rene took off to their West Palm Beach home for a period of total R & R. It was there that Rene developed a renewed romantic interest in Celine. He reverted to the same romanticism that swept Celine off her feet two years earlier when they wed.

As Celine lounged around the swimming pool of their opulent Palm Beach home, Rene showered her with extravagant Rolex watches, leather jackets and other gifts to make up for their recent turbulent months. He was also a regular visitor to Celine's bedroom at night and made a big effort to please the rail-thin Celine, who complained of being sexually frustrated in recent months.

According to friends, Rene gave Celine erotic body massages and lots of love-making, especially during steamy late-night skinnydipping episodes in their private pool.

Rene also exhibited his fetish for Celine's feet, she confided to friends, often licking her toes for what seemed like hours at a time!

As part of this fetish, he also sought out open sandals for her because he loved to see her toes, which he thought resembled those of a ballerina.

Part of this rekindled romanticism was Rene's attempt to try to live up to his promise to get Celine pregnant as soon as the tour was over. But it proved to be an act of futility. Despite numerous lovemaking attempts and widespread rumors in the media that Celine was pregnant, it didn't happen.

Strangely, for a while Celine herself was announcing to her entourage and to friends that she was already pregnant even though she knew she wasn't.

"Celine kept giving hints to people around her that she was pregnant but as weeks passed and she wasn't gaining weight and she wasn't looking like an expectant mother, it became obvious that something was definitely wrong," said one of her friends who had witnessed her white lie stage.

According to a someone close to her, the reason she persisted in telling this white lie about herself stems from the influence of one of her therapists. Celine was told that if she had positive thoughts and acted as if she was already pregnant, that the mental influence would help her physically to become pregnant. But, by the spring of 1997, she dropped this ruse.

Sadly, Celine began telling her close friends, "I wonder if and Rene and I will ever have kids of our own." But she also said that her marriage had never been better and that she was very proud of Rene for trying so diligently to start a family together.

Meanwhile, Rene, who has three children from his previous marriages, admitted to friends that he wasn't all that anxious to have a new baby right away - especially because it would put a damper on Celine's career. He would also add with a smile, "still, we are trying to relax and have a baby..."

A buzz developed in Montreal's rumor mill that, "either Celine or Rene simply isn't able to have children." Celine and Rene's friends realized that the couple had run out of excuses for not having a baby.

"Everybody was starting to think that one of them was not able to have kids," said one close friend.

"It was only a short time ago that we read about Rene visiting a fertility clinic. Something was wrong and it seemed they were ignoring it and just keep hoping and praying that Celine would have a baby."

Earlier, in 1995, several tabloids reported that Rene had gone to visit a Los Angeles fertility clinic. Rumors were rife that the aging Rene could no longer produce kids. Rene's friends say that this made his mood as black and embattled as it had ever been.

But his long-time associate, Ben Kaye, came to his defense. "Rene was so busy during the last couple of years and that put an extraordinary amount of stress on him," said Kaye.

"I don't think there's substance to all those rumors about his not being able to get Celine pregnant. I think when things ease up a bit and they take several months off from the music business, they won't have a problem having kids. I think all the rumors in the press about Rene being infertile have just made him more angry. He already has three kids and he's only in his mid 50's. Lots of men continue to produce kids at his age," Kaye added.

Still by the summer of 1997, Celine's most cherished dream of starting a big family remained just that - a dream.

Celine's spirits were buoyed during her time in Florida by making plans to build a brand new $ 8-million dream home there. This was where she planned to raise her family. Before heading back to Montreal for a sold-out three-show run and a Christmas bash with her entire family, Celine and

Rene dropped a cool $ 750,000 down to secure the land on Jupiter Island, part of Florida's exclusive Admiral Coast. The lot is just a few miles from West Palm Beach and her first million dollar estate - which she was secretly planning to give away to her mom as a Christmas present.

Overlooking the Atlantic Ocean on one side and the Loxahatchee River on the other, Celine and Rene bought the new property in hopes of raising their children there. The new mansion will include more than 60 TV sets and a huge garden.

The most unusual aspect, however, about their dream house is that their bedrooms are to be situated on opposite wings of the house. Celine's confidants say this move was made because Celine and Rene's marriage is currently on the rocks. But the couple insists that their rooms are far apart because of their different schedules.

"Rene likes to start working at the crack of dawn and I like to sleep in till the afternoon," Celine explains, somewhat unconvincingly.

* * * * *

Celine and Rene were apprehensive about her scheduled return to Montreal at the end of 1996 for her series of concerts. Because the US press had been making a lot of her anorexic appearance, Celine knew she'd be in for a tough grilling at her upcoming press conference back home.

So, before flying back to Montreal and meeting the media, Celine did everything to make sure that she looked in top form. She also figured that reporters would be sure to ask questions about her marriage woes and why she was not yet pregnant - and she wasn't happy about the prospect of having to answer these personal questions.

The media had very little opportunity to ever question her directly, so reporters tried to make the most of every press conference where their questions couldn't be censored in advance by Rene.

She and Rene would far prefer the media to stick to asking them pandering questions about sales of her newest CD, *Falling Into You*, which were skyrocketing. But topics like their roller-coaster marriage and her roller-coaster bouts with anorexia scares were far more interesting to some.

Celine and Rene realized that if she didn't look her best for her Montreal appearances, the media would have a field day.

So, Celine went for facials and Swedish body massages regularly at the exclusive Palm Beach Gardens health club, The Spa. There, she'd also get a manicure and have her hair done. She also began eating incessantly in order to gain some of the 30 pounds that her doctors had earlier ordered her to put on.

Reporters were aware of the recent Florida photos which showed Celine's collar bones seeming to stick out like a skeleton's and her cheeks so sunken that she looked sickly.

But unknown to them and to her fans, anorexia had been a thread in Celine's life not only now, as an adult, but also during her teen years.

According to Celine's sister Claudette, their father Adhemar always had trouble putting on weight and often looked very skinny even though he was in excellent health. Celine seemed to have acquired this same trait of being skinny, but in her case, her weight did affect her health. At various times in her teen years, she was given strict orders by her family and siblings that she had to eat or she'd get seriously ill.

A funny point made by some family friends is that Celine's father would probably be even be 25 pounds lighter than he is if it weren't for the regular daily feasts that Therese cooks for him.

A doctor affiliated with New York University noted that being anorexic and being underweight often went hand-in-hand with a host of symptoms which precluded the ability to become pregnant. One of these symptoms was one Celine often complained of - missing her period.

The Dions desperately try not to speak about anything related to Celine's weight because it would be bad for her career to be thought of as having health problems.

Celine did manage to put on some weight before heading to Montreal thanks to the help of Rene, who loves to eat. Celine would play some tennis and swim laps in their pool, then hop into her gold BMW-Z3 convertible and pick up Rene at the golf course. The two of them would head off to fancy restaurants for dinner. He'd take her to places where they could gorge themselves on rack of lamb, steak, fresh vegetables and then luscious deserts. Celine made a conscious effort to put on weight, and it began to show. As they sipped sparkling white wine on those peaceful nights, Rene and Celine looked like newlyweds again, and it seemed as if their marriage was finally back on track.

Rene was pleased that Celine was looking well again and he was even more pleased because he had just succeeded in buying the Mirage Golf Course in Terrebonne, Quebec. He had been an avid golfer for years, and it was his dream to spend his days in the sun playing golf with his buddies when he retired from the music business. Things were looking up.

The couple also began making plans to surprise Celine's family with expensive Christmas gifts upon their return to Montreal. Many Dion insiders say the expensive gifts are more Rene's idea than Celine's because he believes they help deter Celine's siblings from talking about their famous sister's personal life.

"Rene and the Dion clan had an unspoken rule," said a close friend of Rene's. "He and Celine would take care of them financially if they agreed to not talk to the media and to remain loyal to Celine."

The "Too Personal" Press Conference

By the time Celine and Rene finally boarded a plane back to Montreal, *Falling Into You* was sweeping the world's music charts. It had already sold 16.4 million copies around the world, including 1.2 million in Canada, and had risen to No. 2 on the top-200 albums chart in Billboard, the US music-industry magazine. One single from the album, *It's All coming Back to Me Now*, written by Jim (Meatloaf) Steinman, was already at No.7 and climbing on Billboard's Hot 100 singles chart.

At the press conference on December 17, 1996, more than 300 journalists crammed into the Molson Center's restaurant-lounge for a mid-afternoon meeting with Quebec's reigning queen. Also on hand were top Sony executives from both the US and Canada to present Celine with several awards in honor of her extraordinary record sales. The foreign media greeted Celine with adulation and awe. But their hometown counterparts seemed only interested in finding out whether or not Celine and Rene intended to have children. For his part, Rene seemed subdued, and the two of them sat far apart most of the time.

At one point, Celine threw up her hands and virtually admitted defeat, conceding that the "Sabbatical year" she had been planning to take to have a baby was off - because she wasn't pregnant. "There's a lot of time still to have children, even if it's not this year," she said with exasperation.

Celine became visibly more and more perturbed as the harsh questioning continued, and finally she was rescued by her PR representative Francine Chaloult. As planned before the conference, Chaloult finally cut off that line of personal questioning and turned to an English journalist for an innocuous question about Celine's sales and her career. (The barrage of questions had so unnerved Celine that she refused to have another press conference at her next appearance in Montreal three months later.)

Revealingly, when asked if she thought she was the best singer in the world, Celine said, "by no means! There are so many talented people out there. I just got lucky because I have a very well organized and strong team of people behind me. In music you can have all the talent in the world but if you don't have anybody to push, it is hard to go anywhere."

By the end of the press conference, Celine had firmly deflected every question about her personal life into an upbeat answer. "I can't wait till Rene and I start working harder on a family," she said one more time with her rueful sense of humor. "Until I get pregnant, Rene and I will have lots of fun trying to make a baby." This old joke first began on her wedding day exactly two years earlier, says a reporter who was standing beside her. In fact, Celine downplayed the fact that this day was their second anniversary!

It would be a long time before she'd agree to "meet the press" for open questioning again.

And, when asked for an interview while writing this book, Celine's press agent told the author it would be "a whole year" before Celine would even consider it.

The Dion Christmas Bash

Celine and Rene usually stay at the elegant Vogue Hotel on Mountain Street when they're in Montreal. But to commemorate their second wedding anniversary, they decided to do a "repeat" of their wedding night and stayed at the Westin Hotel for a week in the same 29th floor suite they had then.

After her three-night performance at the new Molson Center, (it was her ninth show there in 1996), Celine called her relatives to an early Friday night Christmas party at the Westin Hotel. This bash had become an annual opportunity for Celine to play Santa to her parents, her 13 brothers and sisters and to some 30 nieces and nephews, showering them with every gift they could dream of under the sun.

"It was quite a spectacle," said Sean Rooney, a balloon artist who was hired by Dion to entertain the clan.

"Her family seemed to whiz through the big buffet dinner that was served because they were so anxious to open their presents. It was amazing to see how excited all the kids and adults in the room were to see what Celine had bought for them," he said.

Mia Van Horne, a longtime employee of Celine's, flew

in from France to organize the bash. After dinner, a Santa Claus arrived hauling in huge bags of toys for the kids. Celine personally handed out the bags of toys to each child, and took delight in making the kids happy.

"I've never seen anything like this before," says Rooney. "It was amazing, and everything you'd expect a generous millionaire to give out. Every kid got a huge bag of toys filled with the latest and most expensive toys on the market, like in-line skates, Batman sets and remote-controlled cars."

Celine, who showed little sign of fatigue, was wearing yellow contact lenses in an attempt to relieve her tired eyes from the previous few nights of performing, but nobody seemed to take notice.

Conspicuously, Rene was nowhere to be seen. He was in another room drinking and making small talk with several business associates whom he had invited to attend the party, including Sony reps from all over the world. There was even a Sony representative from Jakarta present.

"Rene should have been there with Celine handing out the gifts," said one of Celine's brothers. "It was Christmas and you'd think he could forget doing business for at least a few hours..."

Before the night ended, Celine shocked her 13 brothers and sisters by giving each one of them an envelope with a check for $100,000.

"I can't believe it," said one of Dion's sisters. "I don't care how many millions Celine is making, she still has a heart of gold. Not many people give that kind of money out to their family, no matter how much they have!"

Everybody in the room was curious about what Celine would lavish her parents with this year. During the previous 12 months, Celine had earned an estimated $100 million.

Celine's brothers and sisters were curious to see if Celine would top her present to of a few years back when she gave Therese and Adhemar a four-bedroom chalet with a built-in-pool in the beautiful Laurentian mountains, along with a fur coat for her mom, and $150,000.

Celine did not disappoint anyone. She stunned her entire family by handing over the keys to her million-dollar-plus estate in West Palm Beach to her parents. She also gave them the keys to her $100,000 BMW. By the end of the night, the waiflike singer whose life had become a fairytale played fairy godmother to her family, by giving them more than $ 2 million in gifts.

"A lot of my sisters and brothers hoped to be successful singers, and I've seen the effort and hard work that went into their unrealized dreams," Celine commented.

"If I'm successful, I do it for them and for me. I'm not the most talented one. I'm the luckiest one because I was there at the right time. I work hard, like a lot of people, but I guess it's my destiny. I wonder, 'Why me and not them?' I've been so lucky, I need to share it," Celine said.

15

Dial 1-800-Celine

When Celine awoke in her Westin Hotel luxury suite, following restless hours of sleep after her Christmas party, she called Rene's room next door to find out what was on the day's agenda.   After letting the phone ring about 20 times, Celine put the phone back down. Rene had already gone to a business meeting, leaving Celine cooped up in her room with nothing to do on the Saturday before Christmas. Celine had wanted to walk downtown with Rene and look at the Christmas displays in all the big department stores, like she did with her mom every Christmas when she was a child. But she stayed put because she was alone.

Sitting in her nightgown on her bed, Celine wondered what had ever lured her into the jungle of the music business.

"Sometimes I wish I could just give up music and concentrate on my marriage to Rene," she would say to friends. "It seems as though I never get to spend time alone with my own husband. Not even to go shopping on the weekend before Christmas. I'd just like to be able to relax in front of a fireplace with kids around us making noise and to smell the aroma of cooking in the kitchen."

Feeling restless, Celine got out of bed and took a sleeping pill that her doctor had guaranteed to be non-addictive, non-barbiturate and without detrimental side effects which might cause it to build up in the body. This remarkable pill had only one side effect, Celine noticed, it did not put her to sleep. However, swallowing a pill made Celine feel calmer, even if it only acted as a placebo, she assured herself.

Celine ventured into the bathroom and brushed her Jennifer Aniston-type hairdo. She then put on pale red lipstick. She never dared to leave her hotel room to start her day before linking up with her husband or at least conferring with him.

One of her band members says, "I often think Celine is afraid of going shopping or walking around on her own. She rarely goes out on her own. And, when I saw how petrified she was that day in England when she was trying to cross a street, it made her seem really strange."

Rene was having breakfast in the hotel lobby with a reporter from the biggest Quebec daily news tabloid, Le Journal de Montreal. He was looking at the details of an upcoming 20-page spread the paper was planning to run about Celine's life. Rene was cooperating because the coverage was the type of splashy gushing coverage he liked best.

Feeling extremely bored, Celine picked up the phone by her bed and wanted to see if her new phone card was working. After dialing, she realized it had not yet been hooked up.

Celine became the first Canadian superstar with her own pre-paid phone card a few weeks earlier. The phone card had actually been more than a year in the creation. Bell was considering launching a whole line phone cards based on well-known Canadians, but Celine's people convinced Bell to do only her first. As far as Rene was concerned, Canadians needed only one image of a celebrity face adorning one of these cards - Celine's!

It was a question of merchandising and Rene didn't think that any other Canadian was big enough to be on a phone card - not even Wayne Gretzky, Shania Twain, or Alanis Morissette.

"Celine is the most popular entertainer on the planet this year," Rene told Bell. "The card's a great idea for publicity, but Celine should be the first celebrity to have one. There's no other Canadian name who is as big as Celine in Canada or worldwide."

Those who buy the Bell Hello phone card with Celine's image across it were able to make long-distance calls after punching in a personal identification number, the same way other phone passes work. These users of also got access to a series of taped messages on her "favorite subjects," including her music, marriage and shopping habits.

Celine's recorded message coos over the phone: "I love high-heel shoes, they're very feminine and sexy, and you walk differently than when you wear running shoes...

"I love cooking and cleaning and being around in my house with Rene, my husband, being in our pool together, just spending some time together..."

Celine thought to herself, shudderingly, about the public announcement a few weeks back regarding the concept of her phone card. Celine had nothing to prevent her from being enthusiastic about the new card because $1.00 off every card would be turned over to her favorite charity, the Cystic Fibrosis Association.

But she was not delighted when she read a paragraph in the press release about how she would be too busy to return her fans' messages.

"I doubt that she'll actually sit and listen to the messages," said Salvatore Lacono of the Stentor phone alliance. "She has people who do that for her."

Celine resented her team of publicists and managers always speaking for her. "Now they plan on even answering my phone messages for me," Celine complained to a friend.

"Soon they'll take me to the bathroom and hold my pants down while I pee!" Celine said.

"I don't know how much more of this control I can put up with...

16

Musician Battles

While Celine herself is always a nice person when she deals with her entourage of musicians, she stands aside whenever Rene acts the heavy. For his own reasons, Rene likes to keep an upper hand with their employees, perhaps having forgotten when he too used to be a paid entertainer rather than a multi-millionaire boss. Musicians complain that he ends up having disputes over petty details with the group, and sometimes leads them on as to when they'll actually be paid for special services.

Lawsuit

On August 28, 1997, Rene, Celine, Sony Music, Ben Kaye, and their associates became the objects of a $ 9-million lawsuit by a songwriter who claims his song was plagiarized. Martin Beaudry of Quebec claimed that a song he wrote was copied by one of Celine's regular Paris-based songwriters, Jean-Jacques Goldman, and then recorded by her on two of her albums, *D'Eux,* and *Celine Dion Live in Paris*. Beaudry's version is called *Your Purple Lips (Tes Levres Mauves)*, while the Goldman version is called *Prayer from a Village (Priere Painne)*.

Interestingly, Rene released a statement only to one journalist, Suzanne Gauthier, a long-time friend of the couple who often acts as a type of unofficial PR spokesperson for them. She quoted Rene in her paper, Le Journal de Montreal: "I have pity for this type of person (Beaudry). He's wasting his time trying to make money and a name for himself this way. He doesn't have any scruples and he has no heart. Other popular artists like Michael Jackson have been the objects of the same type of attack. It's grotesque. He's wasting his money."

But another songwriter who fought for royalties did win a major out-of-court settlement...

* * * * *

Rene was having it out with musician Pete Barbeau in the hallway of a recording studio while Celine looked on from the sidelines. She stood as she often did with her arms folded, leaning slightly back, her sharp hipbones tilted prominently forward. She watched in a trance as long-time band member Barbeau and Rene yelled at each other.

"I've had it with you and your backstabbing!" Rene screamed at Barbeau, who was Celine's drummer for six years.

"I never want to see your face around her again. You just don't appreciate all the wonderful things I've done for you!"

Rene then instructed Celine's head of security Eric Burrows and his team of huge, bulking men who protect Celine not to let Barbeau near him or Celine ever again. Burrows, an American whom Angelil employed immediately after seeing his menacing demeanor at a Madonna concert in Montreal, told his staff to make sure Barbeau or any other undesirables did not get within breathing distance of Celine.

Celine, stunned by the blowout between Rene and Barbeau, broke down and cried.

"I wish we could all work as a team and put our egos aside," she said. "It's all getting too far out of hand."

But her protestations fell on deaf ears, and Burrows, carrying his cellular phone and looking as intimidating as someone protecting the President, whisked the couple to their limo.

"I'll phone all of my lawyers and contacts and make sure that idiot never works again as long as he lives," Rene said during the ride back home.

"He thinks that just because he wrote some songs for us that he's the star of the show. I'll show him who's boss!"

Barbeau ended up having the last laugh. He was furious because Celine recorded a song he co-wrote on the album *Falling Into You* and all he received from Rene were empty promises instead of an actual payment. Barbeau knew the song *Dreaming of You*, which he co-wrote with producer Aldo Nova, was worth hundreds of thousands of dollars as part of the multi-million selling album.

Despite promises to the contrary, Celine and Rene reneged on paying him. Barbeau ended up fighting frequently with Rene over it, and all he got was more empty promises. After the debacle of his firing, he ended up having to threaten Celine with legal action before they agreed to pay him to avoid a public scandal.

Barbeau started out by sending Celine a fat lawyer's letter demanding that he receive payment. At first, Rene told Barbeau that he wouldn't get even one extra penny aside from the regular salary he received as a musician in Celine's band.

Finally, in April 1997, after months of haggling, threats

and huge lawyers bills, Celine's people finally decided to pay so that the nasty affair wouldn't end up in court. They knew it would look terrible if her public thought she was trying to cheat her crew.

Even though many musicians who have worked on projects with Celine in the past, including famous saxophonists Dave Coz and Kenny G., have publicly raved about working with Celine, Barbeau maintains that most of her backup musicians can't stand working for her.

"She and Angelil treat us like second class citizens and we should do something about it," Barbeau often told the other members of Celine's band.

"They only think about themselves and couldn't care less about anyone else."

Barbeau told a friend that Rene's callous attitude was the main reason why so many musicians have rolled in and out of Celine's team over the years.

"Most musicians who've worked for Celine leave because they don't get paid well and they're treated like dirt," Barbeau said to a friend.

"Although she takes good care of some of her lackeys like Mago (Celine's bandleader and keyboard player), most musicians last for only a short while because the conditions are unbearable," he explained.

Barbeau wasn't alone in his criticism. One backup singer who recorded with Celine in the early 1990's claimed that Rene didn't pay her for months, until she threatened to launch a grievance with the musicians' union.

"At that time Rene was hiring all kinds of people who were not union members so he could pay them minimum wage," she said. "He didn't know that I was a union member, and he almost had a heart attack when I threatened to file a grievance.

"I'd never work for these people again because they have no compassion for anyone other than themselves. I don't think that their recording label Sony created a rock star; I think that they've created two monsters!" the singer said.

As part of Barbeau's settlement with the Celine team he was ordered not to blab to the media about how Celine almost ripped off his music.

"I went through a lot but they finally recognized that they were wrong," Barbeau told a friend. "But no matter how much money they give me it can't repair all of the emotional trauma that they put me through. I worked very hard for Celine over the years and in the end I got rewarded with a big headache."

Celine didn't understand what was happening. She always thought the horrible conflict of band members' loyalties could be resolved with a group discussion rather than through a fight with Rene. And, she usually got her way.

But she really was upset that Rene and Barbeau could not work out their differences.

I do feel bad about it because Pete's such a good musician," Celine told members of her band.

"But Pete and Rene are both so stubborn that I have no choice but to take my husband's side."

Many people around Celine think that she is just Rene's puppet and doesn't have the courage or intellect to make her decisions when a dispute arises.

"Just ask her about the constitution," one ex-Sony staffer told The Montreal Gazette in 1997, implying that Celine does not have the brains to deal with anything more complicated than singing or shopping for a pair of shoes.

In fact, one time when Celine went to check into a hotel while Rene was still outside, she couldn't figure out how to do it.

"She didn't even know how to register at the front desk," says one of her close friends.

"You should have seen her, she didn't even figure out that major hotels use plastic cards as keys - and when the receptionist gave her the cards Celine said, 'It's OK - I already have a phone card'!"

17

Celine's Battles with Phil Spector

One of the most frustrating points in Celine's musical career and personal life came in early 1996 during the recording sessions she had with the legendary rock 'n roll producer Phil Spector, who had worked with The Beatles, The Ronettes and The Ramones.

Celine and Rene had huge differences with Spector's recording style. Ensuing battles quickly turned volcanic between the three of them.

As a highly creative person, Spector is a man who never stops coming up with new ideas. He works virtually all the time, mostly at his bi-coastal recording studios in NY and LA or at his large, eclectically decorated house in the Hollywood hills. Spector says he has virtually no personal life; the long intensive hours involved in recording bands make it difficult for him to cultivate one. He spends hours analyzing every nuance of the unsolicited demo tapes he receives. He also thoroughly studies every new video on MTV. All of this is in pursuit of the producer's alchemy: to churn out hits.

When Spector was contacted by Sony music to work on a track for *Falling Into You*, he said he was interested but that he wanted to do his homework on Celine. Spector admits that up until that point he knew very little about Dion's career.

Spector says, "I knew Celine was a singer from Canada, and frankly the little music I had heard from her up until that point did not impress me at all.

"I'm into innovation and breaking new ground and her sound was very pre-formulated and very superficial. If I was going to accept working with her on her new project I needed to do my homework and to see if I'd be able to come up with an original idea."

The idea of Celine's handlers and Sony Music from the outset of *Falling Into you* was to get different heavyweight producers to record various tracks. It was like nothing that Celine had ever done before. Spector would be one of these producers, along with the likes of David Foster, Todd Rundgren, Jim Steinman(Meat Loaf), Dan Hill, Aldo Nova and Eric Carmen.

Spector was worried from the outset that "with all the of the Dion camp's leeches clutching the production wheels" it would be difficult for him to get Dion to sway from her totally commercial style and to try something more innovative. But after catching Celine's performance of *River Deep, Mountain High* on The Late Show with David Letterman, he was sufficiently inspired to work with her. Spector thought she didn't cover the song with the sex and soul of Tina Turner, whom he produced the song for when she did it with Ike Turner in the late 1960s, but he became convinced that Celine had a voice of her own, which was yet to be uncovered.

"I called Sony and gave them the OK,", Spector remembers. "After hearing her on Letterman, it became obvious to me that she was just being manipulated by the people around her. I knew that if I worked with her I'd be able to bring out more of her own voice and expression."

When Rene got word that Spector accepted to work on *Falling Into You*, he was elated. Rene was a huge fan of Spector's since the 60s. He was well aware of Spector's famous rock'n roll Wall Of Sound, his connections with the Ronettes, The Beatles, Cher, Leonard Cohen and many more stars, and his proclivity to turn whatever he touched into gold. "This means millions more albums sold," Rene told Sony Canada's Vito Loprano. "By adding Phil to all these other names we have, it's a can't miss project."

Rene was not aware at the time of Spector's reputation for erratic and sometimes violent behavior in the studio. If things weren't going the way he wanted, he'd do things like throw microphone stands and cables around the studio and sometimes become embroiled in fisticuffs with producers, managers and even the artists.

In 1980, Spector's sessions with legendary punk group The Ramones ended when he pulled a gun on the group in the studio and threatened to kill them if they didn't start doing things his way. Leonard Cohen also nervously joked one day about Spector actually firing his gun at the ceiling of the recording studio during their sessions.

"I do whatever it takes to produce quality," says Spector. "I lost my cool with The Ramones because they weren't paying attention and they were acting as if they were God's gift to music. I pulled a gun on them which I always keep in the studio - not to shoot them, but to get their attention. And it worked. You should have seen their faces, they were finally looking at me and paying attention to what I was doing."

* * * * *

During the first day in the recording studio with Spector, disputes broke out and Celine burst into tears in front of her microphone

Celine demurely said, "Mr. Spector, you have too many fancy special effects you're adding to the recording - like reverb and delay, and sampling and keyboard tracks. On top of it all, the instruments are playing too loud.

"My ears hurt from all the different sounds and I can't even hear myself. I can't hear my voice," she stressed. "It's drowning out me out. My voice gets lost - and my voice is what made me famous. That's what my fans want to hear.

"Rene and my representatives at Sony aren't going to like this at all. I'm the star, Mr. Spector, me. It's my voice," Celine said.

Through her tears, she poignantly addded, "I do respect you, but please don't try and change the way I sound so much, it's not what my fans want to hear. They want to hear me."

Spector's eyes grew wide with fury: Celine was criticizing the very Wall of Sound style that was at the core of his professional career.

Instead of listening to her, Spector hit the ceiling. He began screaming his lungs out. "You're the artist and I'm the producer, let's get our roles straight!" he yelled.

"If your management team does not like what I'm doing, they can shove these tapes up their asses. I've been doing this for over 30 years. That's why they hired me. If you or your team don't like what I'm doing, then why did you hire me in the first place? Let's get one thing straight if we're going to work together, about our roles. You're just the singer and I'm the producer. Please do your job and I'll do mine."

Into her face Spector screamed, "I'm the fucking boss around here - and everybody obeys my every word!

"You're just the fucking singer - and if you don't obey what I tell you I'm going to kick your little French ass and the rest of your fucking mafia music entourage right out of this building!"

Spector's tirade of four-letter words filled the studio, and everyone held their breath.

Celine freaked. The star, accustomed to being treated like royalty in all the big recording studios she'd been in had certainly never been talked down to this way by an employee. By this time in 1996, she was already a huge international star, and everyone usually followed hers' and Rene's directions.

Now, she was faced with this wild-eyed, venom-spewing half-crazed man who was ordering - not suggesting - what she had to do.

She began shaking and breaking out in loud sobs. After a while, Celine bravely tried to regain her composure, and, polite as she always is, she refrained from using any profanity herself.

Clearly she was unable to continue singing her heart out as her fragile body trembled from head to toe. She blindly stumbled out of the recording studio, almost tripping over her own feet and retreating into the ladies' room - and locking herself in for good measure.

Spector, who was still screaming, yelled, "nobody walks out on Phil Spector! Nobody! Nobody! I don't care who the fuck it is!"

He followed her, still screaming, right out of the studio. He ended the recording session and sent home the studio musicians, not caring how much all of this was going to cost

Sony.

Rene, who was schmoozing with other executives in another part of the studio, soon got wind of the fiasco and went to rescue Celine in the bathroom. He protectively took the shaken Celine out of the building and back to their hotel.

That night over dinner, Celine reached another one of her crises in which she saw her career bashing head-to-head with her maternal instincts, and she began pouring her heart out to Rene.

"Rene," Celine pleaded, "maybe this is a sign that we should take a break now.

"I'm 27 - and most married women by now have started to have a family. We're not even planning anything yet. All that we're planning are more albums and more tours and I'm sick of it," she said.

"I need a break and we need to start our family," she said.

"We have enough money - more than we'll even need.

"If we take a break now I could always come back with another album after we have our first baby..." Celine added.

To this heart-felt plea, Celine once again came face-to-face with a cold hard stare from Rene. There was no way he was going to go along with her idealistic aspirations and risk everything they'd gained by slowing down now. As for himself, he already had two children, and, already past 50, there were no new paternal instincts tugging at his heartstrings.

At first, he began responding firmly - but within minutes he exploded. His tone built up into wild fury.

Rene told Celine in no uncertain terms: "How can you be so immature and ridiculous! You're really ridiculous!

"We've worked and dreamed of reaching this point for

15 years and now you want to throw it all away!

"We've finally convinced Sony to make us their top priority and now all you talk about is pulling out of the deal. You can't do it. Not now," Rene said.

"Look at the money Sony's putting into us this week!

"It would cost us the chance that every artist in the world dreams of - to be Sony's number one priority, like we are now.

"And now this - I can't believe you!" he said his eyes wide with genuine incredulity.

Rene added, "we've got to keep going with Phil - but I'm going to come to the studio with you tomorrow. This album will be your greatest ever..."

As usual, instead of arguing and making her point, Celine excused herself, pushed her chair back, and briskly retreating to the washroom.

Alone in the ladies' room, she sobbed for several minutes as she often does during their heated arguments, then composed herself and returned to Rene.

"I guess you're right, I guess you're right again..." Celine muttered, when she returned to the table. She took Rene's hands in hers and added, "yes, Cheri, I'm sorry - I'm sorry." And then, tenderly, she stood up, leaned over the table, and kissed his forehead.

* * * * *

Celine went to the following day's session with Rene by her side. She agreed to try to work things out with Spector. Before the session began, Rene had a long talk with him. Spector listened attentively but told him that anybody who records in his studio must follow his work ethic and regimen.

Rene told him that he got Celine's commitment to do her best by whatever means Spector thought was right.

When the recording session finally continued, Rene grabbed a chair right beside Spector and started monitoring every move the megalomaniac producer made. Spector thought that Rene did not realize that he knew what Rene was up to.

"I've had artists' managers do this to me hundreds of times over the years and always it would backfire on them," says Spector. "I don't care how big Dion was becoming. I treat every artist the same. Rene thought that by making his presence known in the studio, it would make me less inclined to tell Celine what to do. But it backfired. It made me more eager to show who's boss."

Several tracks were recorded the way Spector wanted, but the artistic differences between Rene and Spector became more and more obvious.

Finally, after Rene made one too many suggestions about how Spector should record Celine's voice, Spector turned around and called him "obnoxious." He told everybody in the studio that Celine had been spoiled all her career and that "nobody had ever stood up to her."

Nobody had ever spoken to Rene like this before, and Rene saw red. He immediately pulled Celine from the studio and made a call to Sony's head office in NY, telling them that it was impossible to work with Spector. Rene was reluctant to complain to Sony about Spector because they were so eager for him to be involved in the product, and he didn't want to risk having Sony take Spector's side. But Sony fully supported Rene. They called Spector and told him that the deal with Celine was off. Spector was livid and he threatened to release the recordings on his own. Sony told him that wouldn't be wise because their lawyers would descend on him immediately if he did something without their consent.

To this day, the tapes of the Celine/Spector sessions still sit locked up in Spector's studio. Nobody outside of a small circle of friends even knows what they sound like. But Spector maintains that they're "great."

* * * * *

Months later, *Falling Into You* was released after being recorded under Rene's watchful eyes. As he predicted, it became a huge hit, selling some 20 million copies and becoming one of the greatest successes of all time.

Once again, Rene the genius looked even greater in Celine's eyes - and it was as if another link had been added to the chain tying her to him. It was Rene's genius which had guided the recording, and which had made it the success it was - even to the point where he proved he could beat out the famous Spector. Rene had always stressed that Celine's voice should be mixed way above any instrumental tracks - that was his formula for making Celine's voice become one of the most identifiable voices in pop, and he was right again. Nobody could have done better, not even the great Phil Spector.

Rene had proved once again to Celine that he was brilliant, and that her career was inexorably linked to his visions and dreams - and, perhaps he really was right whenever he said she'd end up as nothing without him.

Celine admitted during a later press conference that she realized it was true that her career was soaring and that her aching desire to become a mother and have her own

166

baby could take a backseat. Her cherished dreams simply weren't the same as Rene's - and so far he had been right about everything.

"Celine was emotionally fragile at this time because she realized Rene was calling all the shots and there was little she could do about it if she wanted to remain married," says a member of Dion's touring crew.

"I was really surprised when Rene agreed to let Celine into the studio with Phil Spector because Phil had a reputation for arguing with the artists he produced. Celine's mind frame was becoming more fragile at this time and if there was a chance of a bad episode with Spector, Celine could have been pushed over the edge of a nervous breakdown," he said.

* * * * *

A few days after Celine finally pulled out of the collaboration with Spector, he sent a three-page fax to Entertainment Weekly writer Jeff Gordinier explaining his side. Spector said the project with Dion collapsed because people around her "were more interested in controlling the project than in making history."

"You don't tell Shakespeare what plays to write, or how to write them," he said. "You don't tell Mozart what operas to write, or how to write them. And you certainly don't tell Phil Spector what songs to write, or how to write them, or what records to produce, or how to produce them."

Rene was furious that Spector made these statements public. He thought the episode was an open-and-shut case and that both parties would not release any details of what happened. "Rene blew a fuse when Spector faxed

Entertainment Weekly," said a member of Dion's road crew. "Celine was in the middle of promoting her new album and the people around her thought that Spector's derogatory comments might have a negative effect. But Celine's publicists quickly downplayed the episode and most people forgot about it."

Celine eventually took a more positive view to Spector's work, perhaps because the artist in her was poking through. She said "over-production" was not necessarily a bad thing because it could be "big time - like *Gone With the Wind*."

She conceded that she loved some of Spector's original ideas, especially when he brought in a 60-piece orchestra. However, she had no choice but to stick with Rene's formula.

Celine added, "Phil Spector would have loved to take a year or two to do an album, but for me an album has to come out fast."

Spector says that if Rene and the rest of Celine's "mafia" weren't present, "music history" might have been made. And, he says he'll still release the three songs he recorded with Celine "when the time is right."

But Rene warns that if Spector so much as plays those songs for anybody, he will take legal action. "He cannot do that without our consent," says Rene. But the eccentric producer says he's not afraid of Rene or Sony Music's threats. "I paid for them and I own them," he says.

As yet, the tapes have never been released...

18

Christmas '96 - Exhaustion under the Florida Sun

Celine spent Christmas of 1996 and the beginning of the 1997 relaxing in the Florida sun. She told Rene that she had no desire to work for quite a while. "I wish we could sit here on the beach forever," she told Rene, as they relaxed. "I'd like to sit here forever with you and just enjoy life... I finally feel close to you again, like we're a real family."

Rene, lying beside her with his big belly protruding over his bathing suit, quickly cautioned Celine that the "second honeymoon period" would soon be over. "I'd like to sit here for a long time too, Cherie, but we've got lots of work to do in the next few months and lots of public appearances. We've got TV appearances on Oprah and Rosie O'Donnell coming up, and you've got to be in top form, my love. These are very important appearances for us."

Celine snapped back, using as polite a tone as possible. "Oh, Rene, we have so much money, we don't even know what do with it! We could stop today and retire and live like the Rockefellers for the next 200 years!"

Rene got off his sunchair and tried to repress his temper. "We must not stop working now because we've worked all our lives to get to this stage," he said. "I know you'd like to have kids now and be a mom with your babies and sit around doing nothing all day. And you will do that one day... but let's fulfil our agenda, please. You've trusted my every decision for the last 15 years, so trust me now. When it's time to stop I'll tell you."

Celine was usually in fear of Rene's wrath and rarely dared voice her disapproval on any decisions he made. Early in their marriage, she often expressed her desire to relax more, start a family, and enjoy the good life. But, due to Rene's constant allegations that she was being selfish and ungrateful about her success, she spoke about these goals less and less.

People who worked in Celine's camp accused Rene, behind his back, of having no patience for people who weren't as consumed with the desire to make money as he was. The accusation probably wouldn't have offended him if he had been confronted with it. Rene accepted his detractors as part of the normal baggage that accompanies those with wealth and power.

"Rene calls all the shots," said a former backup singer of Celine's. "Celine is really down to earth and doesn't see what a control freak he is because he's always saying how he does everything for her own good. She's obviously naïve about the whole situation. Rene is in total control and sticks to his agenda.

"I remember when I first auditioned for Celine's group, she wasn't even present, which is unusual. It was just Rene and Celine's music director Mago (Claude Lemay). I even asked Rene why Celine wasn't there and he said in a really arrogant tone, 'Why should she be here? It's up to me who plays in the band. Celine trusts my musical abilities to choose who joins her on stage.'"

With talk between Celine and Rene once again strained, the couple put their energies into making love instead. Rene boasted that he sometimes made love with her four times in a day during their Florida respite. To those around the couple, it seemed as if sex was used more to relieve their boredom when there was nothing else to do rather than to fulfil any feelings of love.

"It looked like Celine and Rene were taking turns trying to tease each sexually and get the other one going," said a member of their entourage in Florida. "Someone looking in from the outside might have thought the atmosphere was romantic."

"But realistically, it was a manic situation. It was becoming increasingly obvious that Celine and Rene each had different agendas. This made everybody around them very uncertain of the future, from her band members to the people at Sony," said the Dion employee said.

Although their extra love-making efforts relieved the friction between Celine and Rene, whenever they took a breather they'd be constantly flipping subtle insults at each other. Their irritation with each other was palpable.

"If you sleep anymore you might fade away," Rene said with withering sarcasm. He always berating her for her penchant to sleep until three or four in the afternoon. He'd admonish her by saying, "you call yourself a good wife? Well good wives usually get up at seven in the morning and make their husbands eggs and toast!"

The two-week vacation that Celine spent with Rene in Florida was supposed to be a rejuvenating time for her. Instead, by the end of this time her energy level had dropped even further, and she was once again becoming an emotional wreck. Celine started losing weight again and began suffering frequent dizzy spells. One sunny afternoon she didn't even have enough strength to put on her bikini to go to the pool, and began complaining she was feeling ill.

Rene tried to convince her it was simply because of "all the hot sun."

He ordered Celine to go back into their house to get more rest - and she virtually passed out. Just like what had happened at the height of her illness a couple of months earlier, Celine started to sleep for 15 to 18 hours a day. She claimed, and hoped, that resting would once again be an instant cure for her physical and emotional turmoil.

But two days later, on January 13, Celine awoke at 6 AM and started yelling for help. She was in a lot of pain. Rene, sleeping in a room adjacent to hers, woke up because of her screaming and quickly rushed to her side.

"I feel like I'm dying," she pleaded. "Help me, my love, help me or something bad is going to happen to me..."

With the help of one of their housekeepers, Rene put Celine in the car and they sped off to the nearest hospital. Celine checked into the emergency ward of the Palm Beach Garden Hospital where she was admitted for close observation. The doctors concluded that she was suffering from severe migraine headaches, just as she had on several occasions in the past. Celine spent the night in the hospital, with Rene close by her bedside all the time. The next day she returned to her West Palm Beach mansion and, on doctors orders, didn't even lift a pencil for the next two weeks. Rene made sure that he and all the household staff treated Celine like a queen so she could make a speedy recovery. He was freaked out by the thought that she might have to cancel their upcoming mega-tour through Asia if her health didn't improve.

Luckily, Celine once again began feeling well again quickly - but she had lost a lot of weight, and tried to cover this up with added make-up and outfits which made her look

bigger. Her plans to tour Asia were not postponed. And,
she decided to honor her TV talk show appearances.

19

Rosie, and the Oprah Tears

Both Celine and Rene knew the importance of appearing on the huge hit TV program, The Rosie O'Donnell Show, so she made a great effort to appear shortly after her bout of exhaustion. Rene warned Rosie and her producers that his star was under the weather, but they weren't prepared for what was coming.

When Celine showed up for the taping, Rosie and her staff thought they had seen a ghost.

Celine looked terrible. She was probably at her lowest weight ever - under 100 pounds - and she was all skin and bones. In particular, her collar, jaw and cheek bones seemed to protrude from her skin, making her look like an escapee from a concentration camp.

Even her family members were nervous. It seemed as if her teenage anorexic condition was coming back with a vengeance.

When Rosie saw Celine in this condition on the set, she was shocked.

Rosie tried to be all smiles and politeness to Celine herself, but when she spoke to her people off the set she expressed her dismay.

Behind Celine's back, Rosie said, "Celine's so skinny she looks like she's going to disappear..." And, after the taping, O'Donnell added, "the poor thing - I really feel bad for her. She looks like she's either anorexic or like she hasn't eaten a single crumb in weeks!"

"Something really weird is happening with her. I think she needs help...

"It's just not normal!" Rosie added - but she never ended up talking to Celine about it.

The Oprah Tears

Celine and her touring crew had to interrupt her triumphant Asian tour for a couple of weeks in the spring to jet back to North America for several TV award appearances including the Oscars, and for Oprah. Celine triumphed at the American Music Awards, the Canadian Junos and the Grammys. On TV, to much acclaim, she performed her current hit single, an adaptation of Eric Carman's *All By Myself*, accompanied by her band and the world renowned Japanese violin player, Taro Hakase, whom she had hired for the Asian tour. At the Junos, she graciously picked up four awards. But all this was in preparation for her next big challenge - The Academy Awards, where she would end up making Oscar history.

In the midst of all this activity and just before her date with Oscar, Celine had another important gig: Oprah.

The night before Oprah, Celine performed in Orlando and her ferocious schedule was beginning to make her totally exhausted once again. She looked completely drained, as if each step she took was an ordeal.

When Celine left Orlando en route to Chicago where the Oprah show is taped, there was no time for any rest. Her helicopter first flew her to DisneyWorld where she recorded two songs for a benefit TV show to raise funds for the Cystic

Fibrosis fund.

"I don't know how I'll make it through to Oprah," Celine told Rene. "I'm so tired I don't even think I have enough strength to lift a microphone." Finally, Celine finished recording the tunes for Cystic Fibrosis in the wee hours of the morning, and boarded a plane for Chicago. She arrived there at 4 AM and didn't get to sleep until 5:30 AM. She woke up in a near comatose state at 7 AM and was on the set for the Oprah taping minutes before 8 AM.

"Just another typical day in my schedule," she quipped in the limo en route to Oprah's studio. "Boy, I feel as though I would need the next 100 years to catch up on all my lost sleep."

Celine's previous appearance on Oprah a couple of years earlier was a huge success, when she sang *Beauty and the Beast* with Peabo Bryson. She only talked to Oprah for a couple of minutes then, but the two of them really hit it off. Celine told Rene after that taping that she was "amazed at how good Oprah looks compared to what she used to look like." Celine, who often chastised Rene about his hefty girth, told him he could use Oprah "as an inspiration to shed a few pounds" himself! Rene perfunctorily agreed. As a compulsive eater, he often talked about going on a diet and was always conscious about his huge potbelly. But no matter what he promised Celine, as soon as he was around food he'd quickly get a bout of amnesia about his desire to lose weight.

When Celine arrived on the set a big surprise awaited her: her entire family was there as well. Rene had suggested to the show's organizers that it would be really dramatic and touching if Celine's siblings and her parents came on camera with her. The show's producers and Oprah herself agreed that it had the potential to be a real tear jerker that would touch the hearts of millions of viewers.

But Rene did even more behind the scenes.

He always had the viewpoint that when tears are shed by an audience, it makes the cash registers ring like the slot machines pouring out money in Vegas.

First, Rene had told Celine's family not to breathe a word of their surprise visit to Celine to make sure that she would show great emotion upon seeing them. Then, he encouraged them to bring out their own emotions, saying "it's important to let your emotions out, and even to cry whenever you feel like it... it makes the show more touching and meaningful..."

Then, in the limo on the way to the show with Celine, Rene stressed repeatedly to her the importance of her crying and showing lots of emotion herself on Oprah.

"Don't be afraid to cry," he told Celine in the limo. "There are lots of housewives out there who would love for you to break down 'cause they'll think you're more real. And that's what makes them love you..."

Rene also told Celine how important it was for her to try and bring out tears and sympathy from Oprah.

"Give her the sob story about your niece and try to get her to sympathize with you," he stressed.

"If you can get her to shed a tear or two it will be a masterpiece show. Don't be afraid to hug her and even weep on her shoulder. Remember, her audience loves to cry when Oprah cries. Don't be shy, Celine, if you break down it will be one of Oprah's most memorable shows ever!"

As always, Celine followed Rene's guidance splendidly - and his plan worked like a charm. Not only did Oprah cry - but so did the entire audience and the rest of the Dion clan -

and all of it was broadcast on camera. The song that did the trick was *Fly Away (Vol)*, the one dedicated to her niece Karine who was a victim of cystic fibrosis at age 16. Celine belted it out beautifully, putting all her emotional energy into it, as her tears poured out on stage.

Instantly, as predicted by Rene, his master plan was reaching fruition as Oprah herself burst out in tears right on cue in front of tens of millions of viewers: it was perfect. Rene's plans were working splendidly once again.

Within seconds, the cameras began zooming in on audience members who, by now, were crying their own eyes out.

It was a TV triumph, all organized by Rene. And, when Celine realized what a success his plan was, it confirmed once again how important he was for her career.

"Rene's made only the right decisions," says well-known Montreal journalist Suzanne Gauthier, a good friend of the couple who has covered Celine for years. "The one thing I can say about Rene is that he *always* makes all the right decisions. He's a genius at planning."

During the interview segment of the Oprah show, she asked Celine if she was pregnant as several tabloids had claimed. Celine responded with a firm "no" but added that she'd like to have children very soon. Oprah asked her how many. By this time, Celine was having serious doubts that she and Rene would ever have children, but she jokingly replied that she wanted "one more" than her parents had. She knew that was the answer housewives wanted to hear. Even Celine's mom Therese, looking radiant in a red suit, burst out laughing. In a more serious vein, Celine then told Oprah "I'd like to eventually have three children." Before the show ended, Celine and Oprah joined her entire family in singing two old songs written at the start of her career by her mother. These were songs that Therese used to sing to Celine every night before Celine would go to bed when she was a child.

Again, tears flowed freely for everyone.

When Celine finally left the set, Oprah and Celine hugged each other and burst out crying again. Rene tried to show some emotion as well, but all he could manage was a kind of sad look. Inside, he had a huge smile. Not even a demented Hollywood scriptwriter could have conceived a scenario like Rene had just pulled off. Once again, Rene proved his perfect timing and his genius as a decision maker for Celine.

Backstage Oprah could not contain herself.

"I'll never forget this show," Oprah said, all teary eyed. "You sure have quite a story, Celine. This made me think of how important it is to have a family... You're welcome back on the show anytime you want."

After the taping, Celine kissed and hugged her family goodbye. Once again, she rushed to the airport to board yet another plane. This time she was headed to Los Angeles where she was obligated to make a back-up recording of *Because You Loved Me*, the song she was to sing at the Academy Awards, just in case something went wrong during the live performance...

20

Celine would have liked to skip taping the back-up Oscar song as well as the flight to LA because she was so dead tired she was falling off her feet. But The Academy Award organizers insist that all of the show's performers pre-record their songs to televise in case of last minute glitches.

Celine had been nominated for the Best Song category for her song from the Robert Redford / Michelle Pfeiffer movie *Up Close and Personal*. Celine had received so much acclaim for her singing that commercials for the film focused almost as much on her as they did on the stunning Hollywood star Pfeiffer.

Celine did the recording, then finally flew back home to Florida and fell fast asleep in her mansion in the early hours of the next morning. She spent the next couple of days in bed resting for her billion-member audience.

Although Celine ended up losing the Oscar, the show was a phenomenal success for her - much to the chagrin of America's top divas. The fact that Celine, who obviously is Canadian, had such great exposure on America's Oscar's, and also at the Atlanta Olympics, burned up her competitors - including Barbara Streisand, whose song she also ended up singing...

As Celine and her entourage arrived at the Dorothy

Chandler Pavilion for a soundcheck several hours before the show began, Rene was immediately approached by one of the show's organizers to see if Celine would be available to sing an additional song live. This was unprecedented, and Rene was extremely thrilled. Nobody had ever sung two songs in the same Oscar show before. Her luck came as the result of the fact that Gnathal Cole was too sick with a severe case of the flu to sing the Barbra Streisand song *I Finally Found Someone* as planned.

Rene had to convince Celine to take on the additional song. She was so fatigued that she was nervous she wouldn't be able to handle it with her customary excellence. Rene told one of the musicians, "I had to tell her what a fantastic opportunity this was, how the exposure was so fantastic. I also told Celine that the final decision would be totally up to her. Naturally she said yes..."

To reduce her nervousness, Celine asked for a huge teleprompter be placed in front of her during the performance in case she forgot some of the song's lyrics. And, she even brought the lyrics with her on a music stand beside her stool. "I need the words in front of me," she insisted to Rene, "I don't want to embarrass myself in front of so many people."

A few hours later, in front of more than a billion TV viewers, the Academy host Billy Crystal introduced Dion to sing Streisand's song. Celine was a vision of glitter in a slinky low-cut sparkling dress and a comet-shaped neckpiece dripping in diamonds. The Chanel masterpiece around Dion's neck had 656 diamonds. A bright star lay on the side of her upper chest and a six-pronged tail spread down to her cleavage. Toronto sculpture-wear creator Andrea Pope, who created the original design, also designed a costume replica and sold thousands of them after the telecast.

She said, "even though Celine's cost in the hundreds of thousands of dollars, and these were obviously copies, they sold like crazy because people wanted to emulate her.

"The biggest problem I had in my career before the Celine event was that I had no recognition for my jewelry designs," Pope said. "Now because of Celine, people have gone ballistic, and my business skyrocketed."

Streisand declined to sing her song herself because she was miffed at being snubbed by Academy members for not being nominated in any major categories. Also, she has her longstanding stagefright which prevents her from making live performances. But, when she heard that Celine would replace Cole, Streisand was furious.

"How can they do that?" Streisand fumed.

"I could live with Natalie Cole singing in my place but Celine can barely speak proper English... maybe she's not a bad singer, but it's my song. This is too much!"

During Celine's performance of Streisand's *I Finally Found Someone*, Streisand made her highly-publicized snub and walked out of the theater in protest at the Oscar organizer's decision.

"These people make so many bad decisions," Streisand said. "Celine Dion is good but certainly not in the same league as me. I don't think that I'll attend these awards next year. They're a farce."

Hollywood watchers believed that Celine was just an innocent victim of Streisand's snub. Streisand had for years built up an ambivalence toward the movie business and the studios. Most agreed that she would have walked out on almost anybody who sang her song that night.

But even the mighty Streisand had to eat humble pie after her *faux pas*.

Amazingly, a few days after the Oscars, Celine received a bouquet of flowers and a note from Streisand. A Sony executive sternly told Streisand that Celine was hurt when she learned that Streisand had walked out on her performance. He also told her that it could damage her in the long run because Celine was planning to ask Streisand - her long-time hero - to sing a duet on her next album, and that Streisand would make a bundle on it. Celine had done only one duet with a female singer before, and that was with her sister Claudette when she was just 13.

Streisand swallowed hard and told the Sony executive that she might have been too rough on Celine. She agreed to review a video tape of Celine's performance. After watching the tape, Streisand decided to send the flowers and note to a surprised Celine.

Streisand's note to Celine read: "I watched the tape afterwards. You sang my song beautifully and I regret I wasn't in the room to hear you. Next time let us make one together. I really wish your song would have won. You're a wonderful singer. - Barbara Streisand."

Celine was amazed and touched that her idol would write to her this way. She wasn't even aware during the actual performance that Streisand had left the theatre "for a bathroom break," and the plans for recording the duet remained unchanged.

As usual, Celine remained extremely grateful to Rene for scoring yet another coup, and this time at no less a venue than at The Academy Awards. There seemed to be no limit as to what he could help her pull off. Celine told reporters, "I owe all my success to my supporters and family - but most of all, I owe my thanks to my loving and darling husband, Rene."

More Awards

A few weeks later Celine flew to Monaco to accept three World Music Awards. Originally, Celine declined to attend the prestigious Awards' ceremony. But when the show's organizers informed Rene's office that she would be winning several awards and was to be the show's main attraction, he convinced her that she couldn't refuse to go. To ease the burden of a heavy cross-continental voyage, the show's organizers helped arrange a private flight aboard tycoon Donald Trump's private jet. On board were several of her close friends, including Pierre Marchand, director of MusiquePlus TV (Quebec's MTV), who had given her career a huge boost by frequently televising her music videos. As an added perk to get Celine to attend, the show's executive producer promised Rene that Celine would be the only artist to sit at the same table as Monaco's Prince Albert for dinner.

Before the end of the evening, Celine experienced one of the biggest fashion *faux pas* of her life. The netted heart designs around the chest area of her yellow satin dress did not fully cover her left breast. Everybody seated at the same table as Celine and Rene, including Prince Albert, couldn't help but stare at Celine's left nipple that was clearly poking through. Celine only realized this after she excused herself to go freshen up in the ladies' room midway through the full-course meal and looked in a mirror. When she returned to her table she spent the rest of the evening being uncomfortable, adjusting her dress whenever she thought she looked too nippy.

21

All by Myself

Celine spent the next couple of weeks preparing for more shows at Montreal's Molson Center. These shows were being advertised as the last Celine would be performing in Montreal for at least the next two years.

Celine had grown extremely wary about facing her hometown media, and totally refused to have her customary press conference this time around. Reporters had one common theme - Was she pregnant? Was she going to become pregnant? Was she going to take a year off and start a family as she had planned? - and so on. None of this made her feel better, nor did it enhance her image. On top of it all, there'd probably be more personal questions about the recent months of chaos in her life.

It was the type of press situation that even the mighty Rene couldn't control. So Celine and Rene simply decided they could do without the press. After all, these shows early in 1997 were all sold out, so why expose themselves to the media eye? Rene sent out the excuse that, "this series of shows is just an extension of the sold-out series in December, so a new press conference isn't warranted." The Montreal media were furious.

"When they don't need the press they just screw them all. They don't like all that speculation about their baby problems and personal lives, so they just shut the press out," said a Montreal journalist who's covered Dion for years.

Meanwhile, Rene in his fashion was busily leaking stories that the real reason Celine was scrapping her plans for a one year baby-bearing sabbatical was because she wanted to break into movies - perhaps to play legendary singer Edith Piaf in a major Hollywood production. He also raised the possibility of doing an upcoming project with French actor / director Gerard Depardieu.

"Celine and I have always thought that she would eventually wind up on the big screen," Rene said. "With Celine at the top of her music career we both feel that the time is ripe now for Celine to do a major film."

She believed him - but critics who've seen her perform say she's "wooden" and "totally unbelievable" as an actress, and that Rene is only humoring her into believing that he's got greater goals in store for her.

Two Mothers Hospitalized

Celine flew to Europe to wrap up her world tour with a two-week run of concerts that began June 12, 1997, in Dublin, Ireland. All of Celine's shows on this final stint of her tour were completely sold out months in advance. In Dublin, London, Berlin and Brussels, Celine wowed her fans in stadiums that held up to 70,000 people.

But before leaving for this final leg of her world tour, Celine went through her worst trauma ever when her beloved 70-year-old mother Therese was rushed to hospital complaining of severe chest pain. It turned out to be only a bad case of pneumonia, but it shook Celine to her roots. She often said that her mom was the cornerstone of her existence, the one person she could always count on no matter what. The two of them had a totally symbiotic connection stemming from the love and trust they shared with each other. With Therese in the hospital, Celine was devastated.

Therese stayed in hospital for one week, and, according to Celine's brother Daniel, she was "under very close observation and undergoing many tests to find out what's wrong."

Celine and all of her brothers and sisters and her 74-year-old father Adhemar all visited Therese daily. Adhemar was so upset that he too began to feel ill. All this made Celine consider cancelling her European tour.

"I can't leave my mother alone in the hospital," she told her sister Claudette. "What if she needs me? What if she dies while I'm away from her? I would never be able to forgive myself."

To make things worse, Rene's 80-year-old mother Alice was admitted to the same hospital at the same time as Celine's mom - and right on to the same floor. A nurse at the hospital said that Celine and Rene were rushing back and forth between the two mothers' rooms, in a constant state of anxiety. But for Alice Angelil, who was listed in critical condition with a true heart ailment, the prognosis was far more serious than it was for Therese. Her doctors warned Rene that his mother had only hours to live.

"Everything in my life is falling apart again," Celine told a close friend. "I really don't think I'm up to continuing my tour with both of our mothers so sick."

A very subdued Rene firmly told Celine that, "no matter what happens the show must go on... It's too late to start cancelling shows. All the tickets have been sold. We don't have a choice but to go to Europe."

A day later, Rene's mother passed away during her sleep. Celine, who considered Alice Angelil like a second mother from the day she first met her when she was 12, broke down and cried for more than two hours. A friend said that Celine's tears were partly due to the sad realization that if Alice could die, then so too could her own beloved mother.

"I've never felt worse," she said as the tears rolled down her pale cheeks. "After everything seemed to be going well again this has to happen. Maybe I was destined to always have bad luck."

Meanwhile, doctors released Therese and let her return home under close observation. Looking fit and spry, Therese attended Alice's funeral May 29 with Adhemar and the rest of Celine's brothers and sisters. During the funeral at Eglise St. Sauveur in Old Montreal, Celine deeply moved the 300 mourners when she got up and sang *Vol*. Accompanied by her regular backup singers and Mago on keyboards, Celine could barely finish the song. She looked often at her own mother sitting in one of the front pews... she started to weep loudly midway through the song and had to be helped off the stage by the priest. It was obvious that Celine was a mess. People close to Celine wondered how long it would take her to recover from this most recent setback.

"It's a very tough time for Celine," said Rene's close friend and business associate Ben Kaye, who flew in for the funeral from his new home in Nassau.

"Celine was really close to Rene's mom. Alice was always concerned about Celine's welfare, she was a splendid human being. She was like a mother to her."

The Funeral Skirmish

Unknown to everyone else, Celine and Rene had one of their huge arguments right in the limo on the way to the funeral. Celine was nervous about leaving her mother at such a critical time and tried to convince Rene once more to postpone the rest of the European tour. But Rene wouldn't even consider it. A huge screamfest ensued.

Typically, when Celine would try to give him her advice, or tell him that she thought it would be best to take a break, he'd begin ranting and raving, according to an employee.

"Rene would start screaming at Celine, saying, 'you think you're the only female singer in the world with a good voice? You'd be nothing without me! There are hundreds just like you! I drop you and could replace you in a minute!'"

Once again, this tirade reduced Celine to tears. Once again, she totally backed down in her demands, afraid that Rene would really act on his threat and drop her - and leave her floundering just like so many other divas who lacked great management.

Rene's power was even further strengthened in Celine's eyes whenever he was called her "Colonel Parker", as he often was in the hometown press. "Everyone knows how Elvis' career took a nosedive when he split up with Parker, and the exact same thing could happen to Celine," said a source close to the couple.

At one point during the limo ride, Rene yelled at Celine so much that she started to cry her eyes out. Before getting out of the limo and facing a crowd of people gathered outside the church, Celine and Rene both put on dark sunglasses. Celine said to Rene tearfully, "look what's become of us Rene! We're losing our minds. I still love you so much but I don't know how you could still only think of doing our tour and making money at a time like this. Rene, I feel like I don't understand what's happening with us or with anything anymore."

A couple of weeks later Celine and Rene were en route to Europe to close out their mammoth year of touring. From Europe, Celine called her mother as often as four times a day to check up on her.

"I can't wait till it's over," she told Therese one night from Ireland. "I love you so much mom. I owe everything in my life to you. Sometimes I cry at night when I think about how much of your life you have sacrificed for me.

"Please mom," Celine continued, "stay well...

"You're the one person I can always count on. I love you so much... I want to spend all my time with you when I get home..."

* * * * *

Princess Diana

Tragically, the world learned of another death just months later, when Princess Diana was killed in a car crash in Paris on August 30, 1997.

Celine, in a hotel room in New York, was devastated by the news. She stayed up all night glued to the TV, and continued watching the coverage again from early morning the next day. She told a friend that she saw an eerie similarity between the turmoil of Princess Diana's life and her own. It was something she always felt, partly because both of them were thrust into world-wide fame at such an early age, and partly because of Celine's "royal" treatment in Quebec. Celine identified with Princess Diana and her struggles, she told friends.

"It could have been me... it could have been me. I don't want to end up like that," Celine said the day after Diana's death.

"We never know what life has in store for us," a sad and shaken Celine told her friend.

"Something's got to change for me now," Celine said. "I've got to re-think my whole life..."

THE END

About the Author

IAN HALPERIN is an investigative journalist who has contributed to CBC, UP, The Montreal Gazette, CKGM Radio, The Toronto Globe and Mail, BBC, and CHOM-FM.

He is the former managing editor of Canadian Disk Magazine, where he made extensive contacts in the Canadian music industry which proved invaluable in writing CELINE DION: BEHIND THE FAIRYTALE. He also went "underground" for additional interviews to gain information from sources close to Celine.

Halperin won The Rolling Stone Magazine Award for Investigative Journalism in 1986.

He is a sought-after speaker on the college lecture circuit in the US and Canada, talking about investigative journalism in the music industry.

In the past year, he has been profiled in a variety of media including NBC, TV's Strange Universe, CBC TV and Radio, POV Magazine, SHIFT Magazine and The Toronto Star.

Halperin was recently involved in a widely-publicized investigation into the circumstances involving the death of rock star Kurt Cobain, for an upcoming book.